THE ALHAMBRA

A t the base of the hill to the east is the Cerro del Sol (Hill of the Sun). Between the Alhambra and the Silla del Moro (Moor's Seat) and the Generalife is the valley called Aikaibia», now known as the Slope of the Death or of the Rey chico (Little King).

To the north of this triangle is the river Darro, the western end finishing at the Alcazaba and the south "Handaq as Sabika" (the Moat of Melted Silver).

The top of the hill where the Alhambra stands is more than seven hundred meters above the sea level and is an eroded formation of the Sierra Nevada mountains, formed of detritus shist and quartz. Although more recent than some of the formations, it was proper rock, and has by various crystallizations gained the required resistance and stability. If, to this stability, one adds rich ferrous materials in the soil, (reason for the red colour), one can understand why the hill has served as a firm, solid pedestal for the castle of the Alhambra for so many centuries.

Shaped like a boat, it's prow is formed by the Alcazaba pointing towards the city, with a length of over seven hundred meters from the Alcazaba to the tower of the Cabo de la Carrera and a beam of more than two hundred meters at its widest, giving an area of some thirteen hectares and having a perimeter of over two kilometers of walls and some thirty towers, some of them only ruins.

The very recent publication of the book "Foco de antigualuz sobre la Alhambra" (focus of ancient light over the Alhammbra) by Emilio García Gómez,(+1.995) using a text of ibn Al-jatib discovered in Rabat, ('Rooting through my saddlebags to entertain myself in my exile'), has caused all existing theories, solid or eccentric about the Alhambra, to be shaken as if by an earthquake until they collapse in a thousand pieces, and those held to be "profound studies of the Alhambra" by the the Sacred Cows of Arabism or Islamic Archeology, or simple studies of Arabic Art which have arisen in past centuries, all are undone by the evidence of a contemporary of Yusef I or his son Muhammed V, the great builders of the Alhambra.

Firstly, with the new unitary view of the monument we have to throw out, at last, all the functional divisions of Mexuar, Serrallo, Harem, amongst which the Italian word "Serraglio (from the Turkish, via the Persian, meaning "harem" too) is seen as a separate dependency of the private dwelling of the king.

Another point to remember, and often forgotten, is what the Alhambra represents as architecture: this has always been undervalued. We all become tourists when faced with the monument. In the "Manifiesto de la Alhambra" prepared by a group of Spanish architects in 1953, it says 'The Alhambra has never been looked at from the architect's point of view: strangely, even architects faced with the Escorial sharpen their professional eye, when they arrive at the Alhambra, slacken their perspicacity and become mere curious tourists: even to the extent of excusing their complacency by recourse to their emotions: "Yes, I like this, but not as architecture".

Later on the same text they add: "The relationship between this XlV'th century and the most progressive modern architecture is, in some points, astonishing: the human scale is seen in both, the use of organic asymetry in the composition of levels, the way the garden and landscape are related to the building form, the strict economic use of materials, without frills, and in many other ways too numerous to mention".

Thus, the Alhambra, despite its great age, is in concept and construction an architectural complex of great modernity. To quote a modern architect of recognized prestige, the Swiss architect Le Corbusier found in the monument his definition of modem architecture: the intelligent interplay of volumes correctly and magnificently united under the light, an idea established in his "Cité Modeme" (1922). In his buildings he attempts to bring garden and landscape into interiors, and he always uses the human scale as his module.

In the Alhambra, the harmony of asymmetry, the contrast of light and shade, light reducing mass, the focus of sky in the building, water and landscape, the mast and lintel structure, "the agile use of nature in the planning of buildings" are some of the architectural solutions which add to the modernity.

Prieto Moreno, to whom these last words belong, and who was for many years the Architect Conserver of the Alhambra, apos."*the Alhambra combines in its buildings many architectural concepts which are still valid today, and, of course, they are considered masterpieces*". Another

achievement in the construction is the way that the perpendicular axis of the courts is mantained, given the irregularity of the site and the different ages of building. This gives the impression of a regular and harmonic whole.

Francisco Pi y Margall assures us, that the Alhambra 'grew century by century, and every day increased in splendour»'. In effect, the Alhambra was not planned from the beginning as a union of various constructions, rather it grew from the citadel which existed at the end of the IXh century. This sufficed, (in 1238), as the residence of Muhammad ben Yusef ben Nasr, lord of Arjona. When the kingdom of Granada began to grow in importance, that citadel was not sufficient for a real king: starting with the old castle Nasr and mosques, schools, etc. until it became a palatial city capable of housing an increasing and aristocratic population.

At the end of the reign of Muhammad ben Nasr -who helped Fernando III in the conquest of Seville in1248- there was a period of peace based on a truce with the Castillians. At the same time diplomatic and administrative needs increased in a kingdom which covered a territory from Gibraltar to the frontier with Murcia, joined to the sea by a coastal line from ancient Calpe to the river Almanzora, and including the provinces of Granada,

Almería and Málaga, with parts of Jaén, Córdoba, Seville and Cádiz, a long frontier marked by a number of towns still called "de la Frontera".

A century later, during the reigns of the great builders Yusuf I and his son Muhammad V—especially at the end of the later reign—the Alhambra, seen from the Albayzín, was a white castle on a plinth of vegetation reaching down to the nver Darro. This forest which served as a zoological garden where the animals ran free, was viewed from the innumerable windows of the palace. From the farms and country houses of the Vega (plain), then a forest of fruit groves, which concealed a population almost equal to that of the city (according to Andrea Navaggiero), the Alhambra stood out white and brilliant in the setting sun like a flash of golden light on the terraced gardens of the Generalife and Cerro del Sol and at its far background Yabal Sulayr (the Mountain of the Sun and Snow, Sierra Nevada) framed by the blue sky.

But, if the Alhambra was white, why was it called "La Roja", (the Red)? We venture a personal hypothesis, that the name «Hamra» (The red) was given as an analogy of the family name of the founder of the dynasty, al Ahmar, that is "The Red", and this name became common place in the XIV'th century.

The white rendering can clearly be seen on those walls and towers which have not suffered major restoration, conserved areas, large or small, of the onginal finish.

Finally, we draw attention to the use of the name Moslem instead of Arab when speaking of the ancient inhabitants of the Madina al-Hamra'. Arab relates to a certain extent a nationality, and the creators of this Medieval Wonder were Spanish, grand-children and great grand children of Spaniards, who spoke Arabic and practiced Islam; the product of a happy fusion of races who were the founders of a culture which has no equal.

To present this book to the reader we recall the words of F. Villaespesa, from Almería, dedicated to the Alhambra, and which may be seen on a plaque near the Puerta de las Granadas:

Though not even a shadow of the walls remain,
the memory of the place is eternal,
a unique refuge for dreams and artistry.
Then the last nightingale, which breathes upon the Earth
will come to build his nest and sing his songs,
like a last farewell,
amongst the glorious ruins of the Alhambra.

THE GATE OF JUSTICE

Today this is almost the only entrance to the walled enclosure of the Madina Al-Hamra (The City of the Alhambra). It is a square shaped tower joined on one side to the wall which enclosed the aristocratic city known today as the Alhambra, and it is without any doubt, the most important doorway to the monument.

A spandrel of white marble decorated with plaques and strapwork painted green sits above the segmented lintel over the inner arch, where one can see a symbolic key , and below a copy of a gothic Virgin Mary, one can see in a beautiful inscribed panel of arabesque characters: "This Gate called bab al-sari'a was ordered to be put up, may God make the justice of islam prosper and be a sign of His glory for a long time, by the Emir of the Moslems, the warrior

Sultan and Just, Abu-l-Hayyay-Yusuf [...]". This work was completed in the month of the Glorious Nativity of the year 749". That is June 1348, the same year that Giovanni Bocaccio wrote his "Decameron" while isolated in a country villa to escape the terrible "Black Death" which swept Europe and which shortly, like an apocalyptic blow, would reach our peninsula as the "The Great Slaughter" causing massive loss of life in Andalucía.

The name Gate of Justice could be supported by the part of the inscription which says "May God make the justice of Islam prosper within her". As to the name 'Gate of the Esplanade', this refers to the existence of an esplanade prior to the building of the roads to the Generalife and the forest.

The open hand incised on the key-stone of this first arch has given rise to many theories as to its significance. At first, and long ago, the open hand with the palm forward was a sign of peace: it is the natural posture at the approach of an enraged rival. But, in this case, it seems that the significance is in the five fingers, which the Muslims call al-Hamza (the five), that is the five fundamental precepts of Islam: believe in one God, prayer, alms giving, fasting and the pilgrimage to Mecca.

At the level of the roof terrace there are two gargoyles, that in times of war could support a gallery or barbican and in this way covered any blind angles around the tower.

Behind this outer arch, due to its massive size never had any doors, is a separation or defensive wall- typical of the innovative nazarite military architecture-, for hurling down boiling oil or molten lead from above.

This second arch, made of marble, as is the whole archway, was probably polychromed in the Hispano-Musulman period. It is decorated with a shell above the keystone, and another two at the same height at the edge of the spandrels. The arch is decorated with vaussoir, alternately raised, resting on columns with cubic capitals and koranic inscriptions. At the center of the arch, on the key-stone, one sees a key with tassels. This has given rise, like the hand itself, to numerous theories; Hurtado de Mendoza, according Gallego y Burín, opined that this was the emblem of the kings of Granada. One can, of course, see this key and tassel over the nearby "Wine Gate" and over the entrance to the Generalife from the lower gardens.

Beyond this doorway is a horse-shoe arch of dressed stone on half columns, carved into the frame, with cubic capitals. Between the two arches are hung the iron cladgates, which retain their original lock and bolts. We enter under these arches into the access corridor of four right-angle turns in the Almohade style, covered by squinched vaults. These are much in keeping with the military character of the entrance, each turn becoming a point of defence.

On the wall opposite the exit, in one of the niches used as a bench for the guards in olden times, in 1588 the residents of the Alhambra set up an altar for the veterans of the garrison. However, the cisterns were built in 1494. The plaque must have been set up some years later and been nearer to the cisterns mentioned.

Very curious is the confusion as to the name of the Moorish monarch reigning at the time of the surrender, more so given the proximity to the event.

We finally emerge through the rear archway, discovered by Rafael Contreras in 1588. The outer face of this arch still preserves in its spandrels remains of mosaic, similar to those on the inner arch with the niche of the Virgin. They rest on a two centred arch of typical Hispano-Musulman style, and are decorated with a blind tracery of much restored bricks. The infilling of the rhomboids is different to that of the outer gate. To the north side of the gate is an inner moat, which extended all round the walls of the Alhambra at times covered, at others open, but always deep enough to allow cavalry patrols.

The opposite wall, with one's back to the gate, has a rampart which runs from the top of the tower. This wall which seems to have collapsed in the early XVIth. Century was rebuilt with grave stones; possibly from the nearby cemetry of Maqabir al-Assal. or, perhaps, from the Yabbanat Bab-al Fajjarin (Potters Gate Cemetry) which according to Ibn Aljatib *"was placed next to the governor's residence"*, that is the royal cemetry of al-Fajjarin to the south of the Alhambra above the Jewish quarter of Mauror near Torres Bermejas.

These stones are poor material, rough hewn with inscriptions of cufic characters at the edges. Their poor state contrasts with the marble burial stones of the royal family, conserved in the Museo Hispano-Musulmán. Found in the Royal Rawda (cemetry), inside the Palace, coloured and gilded, they lead to the belief that the ones in the wall have a more humble origin.

THE ALCAZABA
(The Citadel).

The Alcazaba, unjustly forgotten by those who wrote about Granada after the conquest, blinded by the Alcazares of the Nazarite, is the embryo from which the aristocratic city (later called *Madina al-Hamrá*) was born.

During the civil wars of the IXth century and the battles against invading Almoravides and Almohades it was known under different names until after the XIIIth century the name Qa'lat al Hamra' (Red Castle) became common place the same as it carries to this day.

From the top of the Torre de la Vela (Watching Tower) one can clearly see two enclosures, one within the other. The smaller inner one is probably of Roman origin, as can be deduced from the foundations visible in the lower part of the walls, and Califal as it was rebuilt in 889 during the defense of this fortress against the Mozárabes and the Muladíes of Umar ben Hafsum.

Even after the arrival in Granada of Muhammad ben Nasr Al-Ahmar in 1238, the Alcazaba was for many years an isolated castle separated by a profound ditch from the area to the east, where the royal palaces were later to be built. During the time of Yusuf I a curtain of walls and towers rose over this, the remains of which can still be seen in the Plaza de los Aljibes (Water cisterns Court); one of these towers was used as a filter for the cisterns which the Conde de Tendilla ordered to be built in 1494, thus filling in the ditch.

(1) Plaza de Armas
(2) Torre de la Vela
(3) Baluarte
(4) Caballerizas
(5) Torre de los Hidalgos
(6) Puerta de las Armas
(7) Camino de Acceso a la Alhambra
(8) Camino de Acceso a la Alcazaba
(9) Torre de Alquiza
(10) Torre del Criado del Doctor Ortiz
(11) Torre del Homenaje
(12) Cubo y Torre de la Tahona
(13) Torre Quebrada
(14) Torre del Adarguero
(15) Jardín del Adarve
(16) Torre de la Pólvora
(17) Camino Militar
(18) Torre de la Sultana
(19) Baños de la Alcazaba

6

King Yusuf I was also responsible for the joining of the royal palaces to the Alcazaba with a wall and inner passage, to which one ascended by a stair which still exists in the Tower of Tahona (rediscovered in 1955 beneath the Cubo de la Alhambra), which is a renaissance construction, pot bellied and with no projection in order to reduce the effects of artillery fire, a weapon which was beginning to be useful at that time.

It would seem that Muhammad ben Nasr al-Ahmar was the builder of the Torre de la Vela at the western end. It has a height of twenty seven meters and a width of sixteen meters. It´s four stories have been much altered to adapt them as living space above all in the lower floor, thus the appearance of the interior is changed and the stairs have been moved.

The tower also lost some of its original height when the battlements were removed, generally due to the disasters it suffered since the XVI'th century: first an earthquake (1522), then the explosion of the power factory in the Darro Valley (1590) -which left it in a sorry state-, and finally because a thunderbolt in 1882 which destroyed the belfry in its original position, the north corner of the tower.

The bell which was recast in 1773, replacing the original one, has the function of controlling the watering of the Vega. On more tragic occasions it called the city to be alert, as when the Alhambra caught fire in 1890.

The excellent view from the tower platform one can see to the north, the ancient district of the Albaicin, and to the east the gipsy quarter of the **Sacromonte** awaiting a promised restoration these last thirty years. Above this is the Hermitage of St. Michael which stands within the old walls of the city of Granada that "pour" into the valley, bearing the scars of centuries. The murmur of the Albaicín can be heard across the brutal roar of the traffic. In the spring time the Albaicin is enveloped by the perfume of flowers which when one is far from the city, still pervades in the memory.

All this is separated from the Alhambra by the **Valley of the Darro**, which extends to the right into the incredible **Valparaíso** (Paradise Valley) which has the perfume of fresh strawberries and the freshness of clean spring water. This is the Granada that Gautier described as "a celestial Jerusalem" and what Al-Saqundi, from Cordoba, described as "a pasture for the eyes and an elevation for the soul".

To the west spreads the modern city. To the south is the Hill of **Mauror** with the **Vermillion Towers**, a most ancient structure which protected the military camp there and the dungeons for the prisioners. To the left of this is the Carmen Rodríguez Acosta, modern, white and cold. Further to the left is the architectural cocktail of the Alhambra Palace Hotel and in the far distance, where the earth meets the sky, is the **Suspiro del Moro** (The Sigh of the Moor) and the last hillocks of the Sierra Nevada, its highest point to the south is covered by snow for most of the year; the

iron coloured foothills are peppered with romantically named villages. Nearer to the east side, stands the stony imperial architecture of **Charles V** and in the distance, at the foot of the Cerro del Sol (Hill of the Sun), stands the **Generalife,** the "garden without equal". There cypresses, like fingers of earth, thrust skywards begging for peace and silence for this landscape.

If one looks downwards, on the western side, one sees a military structure shaped like a Phrygian cap, its point turned towards the river Darro: this is the **Baluarte** (The Bulwark), a XVth century work made as a gun platform facing the city and is the real "prow" of the Alcalzaba.

The city of the Alhambra seems to have terrified the population of Granada more than any outside foe. This is the reason that, finding the citadel of the Albaicín encompassed by the surrounding suburbs and cutting of any escape to the countryside, the kings removed themselves to the Red Hill. Though this required major repair and construction, offered ample means of escape to the outside if flight became necessary, rather than at the western end: the Alhambra was entirely outside the enclosure of Granada.

On the south side, starting from the bulwark, runs the soldiers way which crosses the Bab Handac (The Ravine Gate) which was demolished in 1526 to build the Puerta de las Granadas (Pomegranates Gate). In the same period the Cuesta de Gomérez was opened up in order to give direct access from Plaza Nueva to the central road of what is now the forest of the Alhambra.

The wall continued down to Granada enclosing her within a spacious bailey defended by a number of castles and forts.

Before the building of the Puerta de las Granadas the entrance to the Alhambra began in the Plaza de Cuchilleros (Cutlers Square); zig-zagging through the districts of La Churra and Almanzora, one entered the fortified gate Bab Handac, and along the edge of the ravine of As-Sabika arrived at the Gate of Justice. Until the building of The Bulwark this urban way could have given access to the Alcazaba via a fork to an Almohade style doorway. Filled and uncovered again in 1857, this doorway can be seen near the south foot of the Torre de la Vela.

The **Puerta de las Armas** (Gate of Arms) which is the true main gateway to the Alcazaba, was equipped with a portcullis, its raising and lowering controlled from the floor immediately above the entrance. One reached there along the walled road of the Alcazaba: this tower is attached to the bailey of the Alcazaba and next to the Vela. The entrance to the Torre de la Armas is a wide passage which turns sharp right to meet a large space (certainly the guardroom) where the way opens in two directions: one to the left leading to the royal palace and the other to the right which gives entry to the Alcazaba.

The visitor to the royal residences (whether on horse back or on foot) was required to go some ninety meters with his right side exposed to the crossbowmen on the inner wall— the shield was borne on the left side—. Passing first a gate, since demolished, one came to the next point of control at the Torre de la Tahona and then to a market or zoco (its remains can still be seen) which was held by tradition in the entrance of all fortified cities.

At the end of a pebble paved slope our visitor arrived in the Plaza de las Armas. Before his gaze was now a central street with a bath house for the soldiers to his left. On both sides were houses for the officers of the garrison, armorers, blacksmiths etc, the foundations of which are still to be seen. There are also water cisterns, ovens and a dungeon.

This Plaza de las Armas is enclosed by the following towers, starting from the Torre de la Vela: **Torre and Puerta de las Armas, Alquiza, El Criado del Dr. Ortiz** (The servant of Dr. Ortiz), and in the north west corner, la **Torre del Homenaje** (The Donjon), similar in height to the Torre de la Vela and irregular in plan (12.12 x 10.45 mts.). Its five floors, including the cellars, served first as the residence for the wardens and then as a prison for Algerian pirates and francophiles.

The Torre del Homenaje is one of the oldest in the Alcazaba, dating from the period of the Caliphate. An archaeological study of the materials of which it is constructed compared with those at its base, leads one to think that perhaps Al-Ahmar ordered it to be rebuilt on the ruins of a tower dating from the ninth century. After the Torre del Homenaje comes the **Torre Quebrada** (Cracked Tower) so called because of the long crack to be seen from the Plaza de los Aljibes, looking like a wound from head to toe. It is solid to the top of the wall, having two floors above this level.

Next comes the **Torre del Adarguero** (Leather-shield Maker) of which only the shell remains. To the right of the Torre del Adarguero is the former entrance to the Alcazaba which leads directly to the Jardín del Adarve. This garden is the old moat which divided the inner and outer baileys and was filled in with rubble and earth in the early XVlIth century by the Marqués de Mondéjar, to make the garden. The original moat depth can be imagined by observing the height of the cypresses planted at the foot of the outerwall.

On the inner wall there were two small towers, of which only the **Torre de la Sultana** remains. Through this garden going west, one reaches the **Torre de la Polvora** (GunpowderTower) which marks the start of the above mentioned Camino Militar to Torres Bermejas. From here, through another small tower, one enters the Torre de la Vela by a modern entrance at the level of the second floor.

From either the Adarve gardens or from the Torre de la Polvora the view is so spectacular that any description can only diminish it.

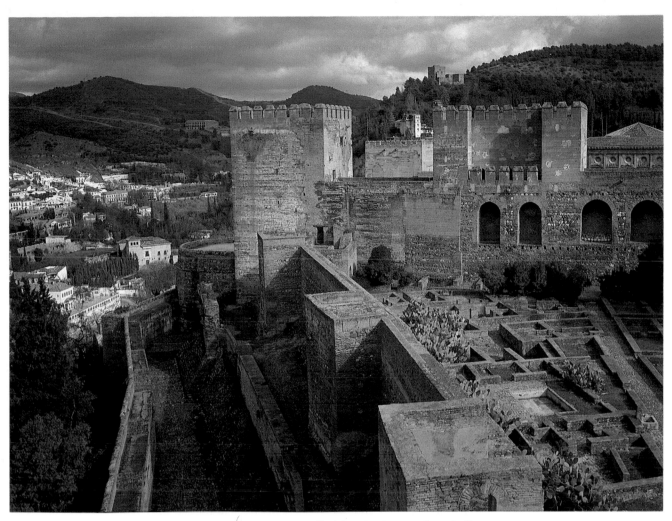

La Alcazaba — The Fortress — Citadelle — Die Festung — Rocca fortificata

Albaycín

Bosque de la Alhambra — The forest — Le bois — Der Wald — Il bosco

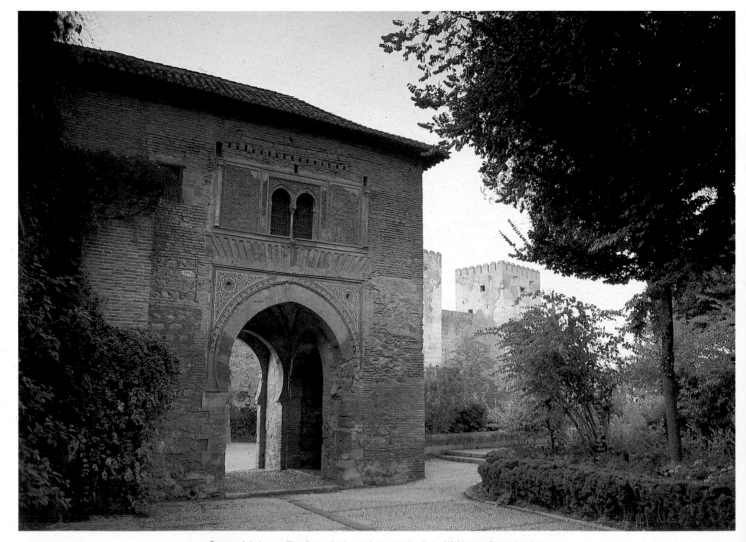

Puerta del vino — The Gate of wine — La porte du vin — Weintor — Porta del vino

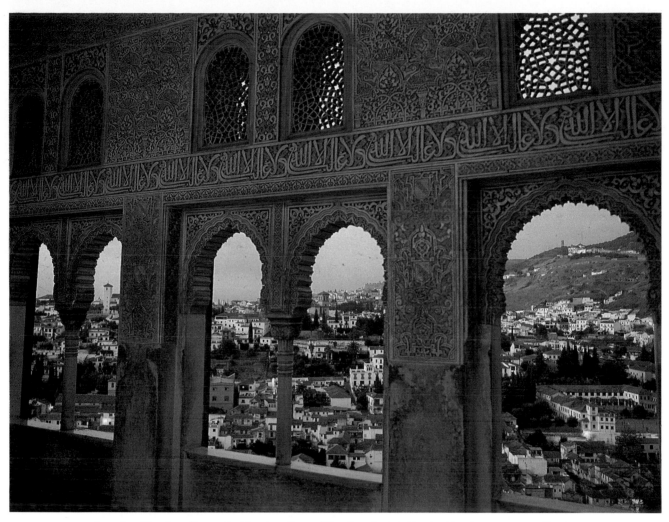

Oratorio y Albaycín — View on the Albaycín — Vue sur l'Albaycin — Aussicht über den Albaycin — Moschea e l'Albaycin

Mexuar

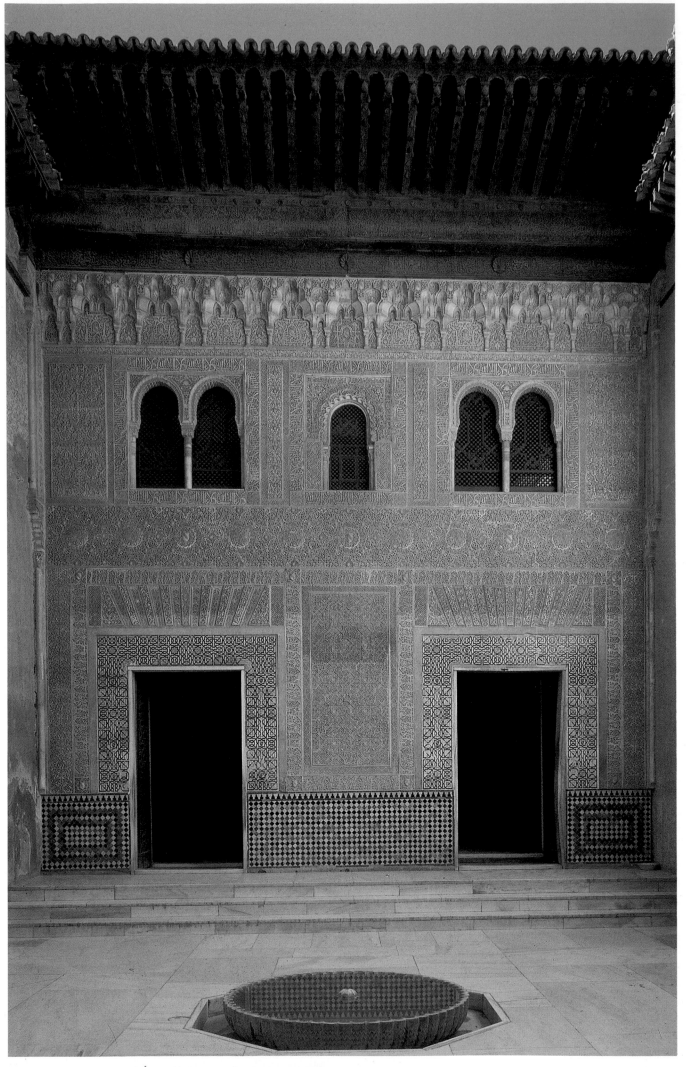

Fachada de Comares — Façade of comares — Façade de Comares — Hauptfassade von Comares

Patio de los Arrayanes

THE OLD ROYAL PALACE

THE HALL OR ROOM OF THE MEXUAR

This is the part of the palace which has suffered most from conversions, almost always at the instigation of the Christian Governors in the service of their King, adapting it to new uses and functions, drastically altering the original appearance. These changes have meant the complete destruction of old structures, making it difficult to identify the original entrances to this part of the palace, where it seems the council met to decide important judical mattrers.

Those approaching from Granada, once they passed the filter of the Alcazaba and the control of the Tahona Tower, found themselves in a town square, or Zoco, a typical feature of town entrances (the Alhambra was a town). They then passed into a higher courtyard and finally they reached the Court of Machuca.

This court is so called because of the Machuca Tower on the side facing the River Darro, where the architect of the Palace of Charles V., and his son Luis (also an architect) lived. On the opposite side was a twin of this gallery but only some ruins on the floor remain. Its original form is recalled by some cypress arches.

The entrance to the buildings was very similar to the present one. A flight of ruined stairs at the end of the cypress gallery seems to confirm this. In the small upper court we find the entrance to the Hall of the Mexuar. This doorway, with its fine carved surrounds was, brought from some other location.

THE MEXUAR

This room, commonly called the Mexuar is probably the oldest part of the royal apartments to survive, even if it was much altered in the time of Yusuf I and his son Mohamed V. In a frieze of a what was a roof light at the centre of the room, one can read *"Glory to our lord Abul-Walid Ismail"*. This and its similarities to the Generalife, built and decorated by this King, leads to the belief that it was built in the early XIV'h century.

In plan there is a notable disproportion between the areas divided by the central columned area, the northern end, between the columns and the entrance being much the

25

larger. In this room a chapel was installed. As the room was found to be too small the end was demolished and a choir gallery built in the space gained with the pick.

In a recent excavation a small court with clay paviours was revealed under the choir gallery, proving that the room was enclosed at this side. The Mexuar was isolated from those whose business in the palace was not related to it.

The four columns at the centre of the room indicate the location of a roof lantern. It would have had clerestory lights on all four sides, filtering the daylight through coloured glass. Below this, in the square formed by the four columns, the Council met to decide important judicial matters. In the doorway there was a tile which said : *"Enter and fear not to ask for justice, for you will find it".*

When the warden's residence (now the Hispano-Musulman Museum) was built above, the lantern was destroyed. The square space which remained, enclosed by the four columns, was covered with a radial wooden ceiling.

The west wall was thickened to take the extra weight, and the large, iron grilled windows which now light the room were opened in it.

The room was extended to include the small court. In the dividing line a choir Gallery was built, supported by a decorated beam resting on Arabic columns, with their bases sunk in the floor. To this was added a wooden railing and two more columns of the same style which reached the ceiling. The Moorish Oratory behind was used as a sacristy.

Despite all these viscisitudes the upper part of the walls of the hall conserve the original colour and gilding of the plaster decoration, and some of the wooden ceilings are original, recognisable by their polychroming and darker colour.

Above this work in ceramics (which lacks the brightness of the work it imitates), the length and breadth of the room we can read the litanies "The power of God", "The glory of God" and "The kingdom of God".

A plaster imperial crown can still be seen over the doorway, but the other one remains as it was on top of the column.

THE ORATORY OF THE MEXUAR

It was one of the parts of the Alhambra which suffered most damage from the explosion of 1590, so much so that it had to be completely rebuilt at the time, this work being completed in 1917.

On any plan of the Alhambra one can see that the Oratory does not follow the line of the walls; it angles sharply to the south east, seeking orientation towards Mecca for the Mihrab.

There are some inscriptions around the Mihrab, that says, *"Be not neglectful, come ye to pray",*

THE COURT OF THE MEXUAR

This is a small court which, for no apparent reason, was called "The Court of The Mosque", in days gone by. On the north side is the Cuarto Dorado and opposite the impressive front which has been held until now to be the entrance to the Palace of Comares.

One has only to see the many engravings of this court made in the last century, to lose any reticence about the work of the restorer. In this case the restorations are numerous and well executed.

The court centres on a fluted, white marble fountain. This is a replica placed there in 1943 to fill the hole left by the removal in 1626 of the original one used as part of the Christian fountain in the Court of Lindaraja.

The demolition of a Morisco arch and the removal of the projecting floor which it supported has restored the former attractiveness of the Cuarto Dorado gallery. This gallery is composed of three well proportioned arches which rest on white marble capitals, possibly Almohade in origin. These in turn rest on slender white marble columns. The capitals are a stylised version, inspired by the zoomorphic capitals of Persepolis.

The Cuarto Dorado (Golden Room) beyond the gallery opens onto the woods through a Gothic window, divided by a mullion on whose head are the emblems of the Reyes Catolicos (Catholic Monarchs). The restoration dates from their reign and the original ceiling was preserved but redecorated with Gothic motifs. The ceiling rests on a frieze containing the emblems and motto of the royal couple.

On the eastern wall of the court is a tunnel which leads to the Baths of the Palace of Comares it has rooms on bothssides, once used as quarters for the guards and now used to store the results of the excavations being carried out in the Alhambra.

THE FAÇADE OF THE PALACE OF COMARES

To many authors this façade, on the south wall of the court, deduces the "existence of some architectural or decorative element in the court, to give the correct orientation". It is clear that this façade, intended as the entrance to the Palace of Comares, is far too monumental for this small dark courtyard .

A study of the manuscript by Ibn Aljatib, discovered in Rabat has lead don Emilio García Gómez to surmise that this façade, together with its doors, was originally sited on the southern side of the Patio de los Arrayanes and that it was the principal entrance to the Palace de Comares, but on the outside.

Later, through the records of building works in the Archivo de la Alhambra, he shows that in effect it was moved between 1537 and 1538 to its present location.

However, in Machuca's plan one sees two doors, which confirms Graber's hypothesis on the "existence of some architectural or decorative element to give the correct orientation".

The façade stands on a plinth of three marble steps and the moulded plaster decoration increases in complexity as it rises, perhaps in imitation of the classical orders. It finishes with finely carved, overhanging eaves, a fine work of carpentry, and rests on a frieze of the same material where decoration is no less perfect than the eaves or the rafters that support it.

This façade, much restored in the nineteenth century, has dividing strips between the decorative panels. There is an abundance of Magrebies characters surrounding the ajimez windows at the sides and a central window where we see repeated the dynastic motto:

"Only God is Victor".

In the frame around the doors, including the plaster jambs and the panel between the two, one can see various religious themes taken from the Koran written in cufic characters.

Above the lintels of the doors we can see the remains of the original tiling which has been continued in modern stucco down the jambs to the tile dado at the foot of the wall, also restored .

The aesthetic impression of this façade, wherever it was, must have been very moving: polychromed like a Persian carpet, with the mouldings and the eaves gilded, the polished bronze doors also looking like gold.

The right hand door leads to a post-conquest lobby, to some other Christian buildings and finally to the exit from the Arab palace. The left hand door leads to a small room with its ceiling and frieze gilded in the time of the CatholicMonarchs. Here in Gothic characters it erroneously says that Granada was conquered one year before it actually was (in 1492). At the end of its angled corridor we reach the Patio de los Arrayanes.

COMAREX

This complex containing the Hall of Ambassadors or the throne room is the most important of all the buildings in the Alhambra. The austerity of its design and the balance of its proportions fills the court with a serene majesty, so that one can breathe in the noble grandeur of the kings who built it.

The proportions are just perfect, so much so that when attempts are made to copy them on a smaller scale the effect is paltry, not to say ridiculous.

The Court of Myrtles was the centre of the diplomatic and political activity of the Alhambra, and probably the place of state reception for foreign ambassadors. It would be the place where important visitors would have awaited their turn to be received by the Sultan.

Until now the whole building has been attributed to Yusuf I. Despite the presence of a eulogy to Muhammad V on the north gallery celebrating his reconquest of Algeciras all the building works belongs to his father's reign. However in Emilio Gómez's study of the aforementioned manuscript by Ibn Al-jatib it is made clear that the Court of Myrtles belongs to the period of Yusuf I.

It was in fact an open esplanade with a central pool. It was left to Muhammad V to enclose this esplanade, converting it into a monumental courtyard and preserving the northern buildings put up by his father, i. e. the gallery and Hall of the Ambassadors as well as the royal baths bellow the Palace.

The medieval visitor who entered from the south, having passed through the main entrance, found before himself a huge mirror of water reflecting the white mass of the Tower of Comares and, due to the slope of the white marble floors which permitted the water to reach the bases of the columns on the north side, these appeared to float on the water. All the buildings on this side including the tower became floating palaces. Thus when the rest of Europe was building "castles in Spain, in Granada they built palaces on the water". The most important function for the pool was that of a mirror, a feature used centuries later (1630-1647) in the well-known Taj Mahal in Agra (India).

If we suppose that the proponents of the theory about the entrance to The Hall of Comares are correct, the present entrance would have been a secondary entrance from the rooms in the Mexuar, never the solemn entrance to the residence of a king that one would expect.

On many occasions it has been stated that there were no tiled dados along the side walls but that there were some flower beds at their bases in which jasmin and roses grew. One only has to see the cut-away shape on the lower part of the door surrounds to see that there was a tiled dado at that level.

Richard Ford tells us that the daughters of Bucarelli tore down the ceramic tile surrounds that ran the entire length of the court and sold them off.

The south wall has a very recent ceramic dado copied from a sixteenth century one in the north gallery. This is a colonnade of seven arches covered by a seven domed ceiling of "lazo" (strap-work). At the east and west ends are another two takas, the western one being a modern reconstruction. The central arch of the gallery is higher than the others and rests on two capitals of Mocarabes in the style of Ispahan. Three others on each side are supported by cubic capitals.

Of the two doors which once existed on each side of the south wall only the one in the east corner with its plaster arch still stands, and leads by some stairs to the upper floor.

Behind the central arch is the so called "crypt of the Emperor's Palace". It is reached through the remains of a room severed diagnonally by the stones of the renais-sance palace. This room was similiar in its shape and size to the Sala dela Barca, although not so high.

The inside of the arch which leads to the crypt -of which we will write later- is adorned with foliate decoration in delicate tones of blue and above the arch are three windows with plaster jalousies. Above the roof of this gallery there is a long room which has seven windows opening onto the court (the central one, an Ajimez) and all have modern wooden jalousies. This long room which connects with the upper part of the Court of Lions was a concession to the women of the household, a form of discreet observation gallery from where they could watch the goings-on in the court without being seen.

There is a third floor above this last room. This is a seven arched gallery with a lazo ceiling. The central arch has a straight lintel, higher than the others and resting on decorated hammer beams. All the voids of this upper gallery are closed off by wooden jalousies in the form of a parapet and which were made in the last century.

The plaster inscriptions of the southern portico are principally praises to God with a few dedicated to the Sultan. They are mostly copies of those at the north end.

Each of the buildings on the long sides of the court has five doors. On the west side the first door (south end) was used as the main entrance to the court for a long time, and the last door on this side (north end), next to the present entrance, communicates with the upper floor via a staircase where the Hispano-Musulman Museum is situated.

The first door on the east side (at the southern end) has connected since the Christian occupation with the Court of Lions and with the eastern doorway of the Palace of Charles V. The last door on the east side (northen end by the gallery) was the original entrance to the Baths of Comares. All these edifices, for which the exact functions are not known, have two floors. The upper ones are lit from balconies with ajimez windows. The presence of platforms made of brick on the floors of some of the rooms has lead to them being written about as the women's quarters. However the civil servants of the time worked sitting on low daises and the women lived in the Court of Lions.

The North Gallery has great similarities with the southern one because many of the decorative elements and epigraphs are copied from the northern one, which we shall now describe.

It has the same number of arches and the same layout of supporting members on capitals. The large central arch rests on Isphahan type capitals and the rest on cubic ones. The ceiling of this gallery together with part of the Sala dela Barca (Hall of the Boat) was destroyed in the fire of 1890 and masterfully rebuilt later reusing many of the surviving burnt pieces.

LA SALA DE LA BARCA

The greeting Baraka (a blessing) appears everywhere. It was the repetition of this word in the Sala de la Barca which seems to be responsible for its name by corrupting the phonetics. Considering also the similarity between the ceiling and a upturned boat, "barca" in Spanish, the name is all the more justified.

In the jambs of the entrance arch there are some finely sculptured marble niches which were used to hold jars of water, perfumes or flowers. Almost always water was a symbol of hospitality, as one gathers from the translation of the poem about the niches.

The gold coloured ceramics of the dado date this construction to the first half of the fourteenth century. The ceiling, a semicylindrical vault, was destroyed in the fire of 1890 but the present one which was built in 1965 compares favourably with the original.

The direct entrance to the Hall of the Ambassadors is under a large arch. Beyond this there are two narrow spaces. The lefthand one has a small door through which one can reach the different floors of the tower—these stairs offer a wide variety of vaulting on each landing and the right hand one is a small oratory where the Mihrab has been turned into a window giving light from the Patio de Lindaraja.

In the jambs of the next arch are two more small niches with verses in finely worked plaster giving clear reference to the water they contained, as on the right hand one where it says: *"The jar of water within me is like the faithful one in the quibla of the temple who remains absorbed in God... giving relief to those who thirst"*. In the left hand one it says: *"Whosoever comes to me thirsting I will lead him to a place where he will find clean water, cool, sweet and unpolluted"*. One can still see the remains of the gold leaf in the hollows of the mocarabes of this arch, and in the niches or takas are the remnants of the polychroming.

THE HALL OF THE AMBASSADORS:

Remain magnificent even though stripped of its stained glass windows which were lost in the explosion of 1590. This stained glass was a continuation of the design in ceramics on the dado, with the same geometry, where the fine lines interlaced in the ceramics were repeated in the lead fillets which held the coloured glass. The daylight was tinted by these colours and was cast onto the blue and gold floor tiles of which a few remain in the centre of the room, fenced off by chains.

Not all the tiles thus protected are original. The few that are, are the ones where the blue glaze and the royal shields they surround are smooth, not with raised edges between the colours to hurt the feet as in the more modern copies made after the reconquest and amongst which the originals are dispersed.

This room is a square of 11.30 metres each side, with three openings 2.50 metres deep on each side -this being the thickness of the walls of the tower- the centre window being an ajimez and the ceilings fine wooden "artesonados". The windows, which open to the north, east and west have two small windows above each. Almost at the cornice which supports the splendid ceiling there are five windows on all four sides which are reminiscent of desert architecture. Those on the south side have been filled in as a means of reinforcing the wall against collapse. The central window ledge on the north side was the throne, according to the inscriptions on the wall above the tiling in this area where it says, "(...) *Yusuf* (...) *chose me to be the seat of the kingdom. The lord of this kingdom makes it a great and divine throne*".

From this position the Sultan exercised a certain psychological hold over the citizens of the capital who at the same time would have felt themselves under the gaze of the religious, political and military head of the kingdom.

From the moment they entered the doorway of the Sala de la Barca, the ambassadors would have felt intimidated by the silhouette of the Sultan seated against the light of the stained glass and looking upon them as they advanced across a sumptuous scenario of brilliant colours and sparkling gold.

Before the southern windows were filled in, the Sultan would have been able to sit or lie on his throne and simultaneously enjoy the view of the city with its gardens, and the reflections of the windows and sky on the water which lay before his eyes in the Court of Myrtles.

The ceiling is the masterpiece of the carpenters of the kingdom. It rests on a cornice of painted wooden "mocarabes" where one can read the Sura LYVII of the Koran or the Kingdom. In the third Aleya it says, "*He did make seven heavens one above the other; no discord will you see in this pious creation*".

This is a clear reference to the seven heavens spoken of in the Koran in three of its suras , surely referring to the design on the ceiling of the room.This is made up of 8,017 pieces of wood with superimposed reliefs in cedar and made into various symmetrical panelsframed in a boss of mocarabes at the top of the dome.

Don Darío Cabanelas found a plaque showing the colours to be applied to this ceiling, white, red, walnut-white, light green, red, green and once again red in that order.

Amongst all the cufic, magrebie and hispano-cursive characters which include religious themes, the constant repetition of the device "Only God is the Victor" and the praises to Yusuf I (and one must be impressed by the decorative value of the Arabic epigraphy) and just visible on the capital of one of the niche arches, is a text indicating the public nature of the hall. Begging brevity, it says:

"*Few words and you will leave in peace*"

Sala de Dos Hermanas — Hall of the two Sisters — Salle de Deux Soeurs — Raum der Zwei Schwestern — Salla delle due Sorelle.

Patio de los Leones: Detalle — Detail — Détail — Detail — Particolare

Partal

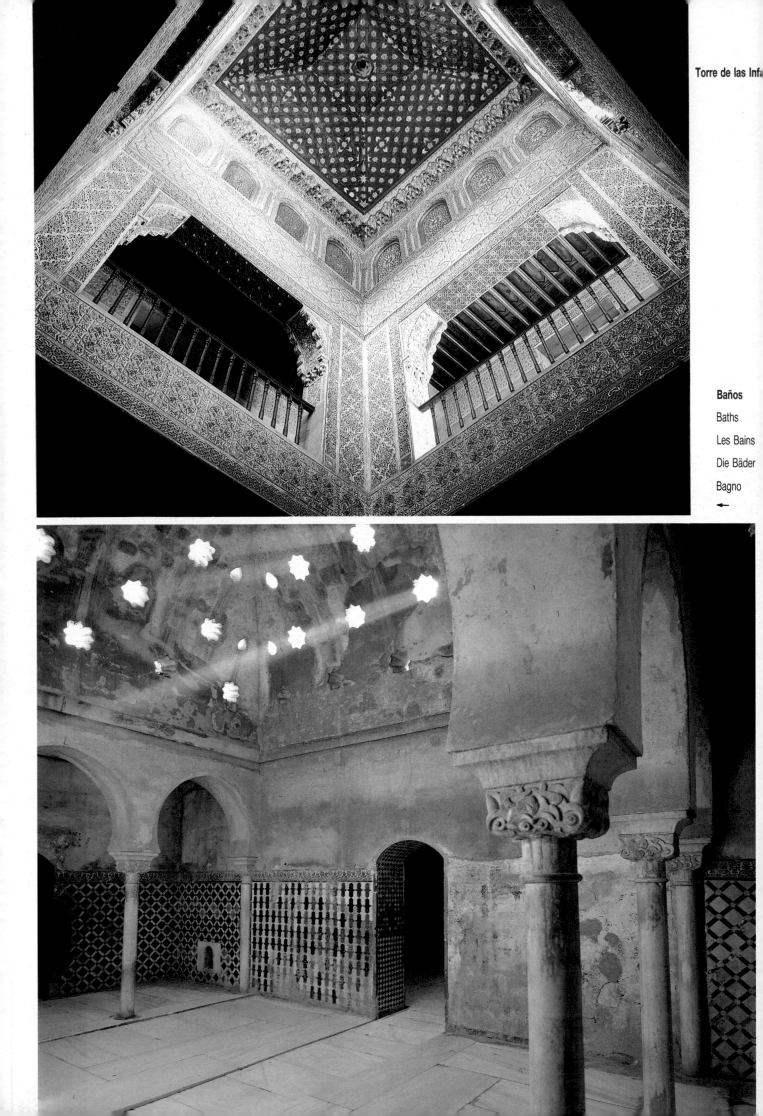

Baños
Baths
Les Bains
Die Bäder
Bagno
←

Torre de las Infantas

Mirador de Lindaraja

Sala de los Reyes

Sala de Dos Hermanas

Sala de Abencerrajes

Manolo Castillo

THE COURT OF LIONS

This was the centre of the Sultan's household and included the area given to the women of the royal house. It cannot be called harem for its function was not exclusively feminine in nature, as it was also used for activities related to diplomatic and political life of the kingdom.

We know now that on the 30th December 1362 the Court of Lions consisted of no more than the Hall of the Two Sisters and the buildings that now enclose it were erected after this date. The entrance was through a small door in the southern corner of the court and it leads into a small lobby which still contains remains of fine foliate decoration and benches for the guards.

As you passed through the entrance to the Court of

Lions, its beauty unfolded again little by little whichever of the two paths the colonnaded cloister directed you. A forest of golden columns opened up before the visitor and, continuing slowly along, resembled "*the golden fringes of a spread of lace suspended from the sky*", because the garden plants in the middle prevented you from seeing how the pillars rested on their marble bases.

The uniformity of capitals and arches is only illusory since there is great decorative diversity which is not apparent at first. The shafts of the columns are joined to the bases and capitals by lead joints so that reasonable thermal movement can be accommodated and a perfect assembly could be achieved for the three elements.

The shorter two sides of the court are not symmetrical either. On the east side on each flank of the prominent pavilion the columns stand in two pairs and a single one, whereas on the opposite side are two single columns and one pair on each flank. On the east and west sides of the court are two pavilions which intrude into the quadrilateral, each with a small fountain. The coffered ceilings of these pavilions are beautiful wooden domes which still conserve some of the original polychroming. These are two perfect hemispheres made with flat components. The western pavilion has its roof built above the original cornice and the intervening space is decorated with imperial eagles in plaster, recalling the period when its height was altered. This change in height is not entirely capricious, but a consequence of the difference in the line of sight between a man seated on the floor or lying down and another man standing up.

In the centre of the court the Fountain of the Lions sprays water and refreshes the atmosphere through the mouths of twelve white marble lions, which as they stand in a circle watch over every hook and cranny of the court. On their backs they carry a dodecagonal (twelve-sided) bowl and on its sides one can read a qasida by Ibn Zamrak which apart from being beautiful, explains many of the details of the court and of the fountain. Are these the same gilded copper lions which Ibn Aljatib saw before the court was built? The theory nevertheless exists that the lions were once polychromed and there is evidence that they have been scraped.

This court with its arches of perforated tracery forming rhombuses and its colonnades of fine pillars seems inspired by the Cistercian cloisters of the period, a theory aided by the fountain in the centre of the court. The rooms at the sides of the court are joined to the Lions Fountain by a sort of marble cross. Along its canals the water flows from the fountains to the halls of Abencerrajes and the Two Sisters and from the centre of the two pavilions.

THE HALL OF THE MOCARABES

This is the first room as one enters from the Court of Myrtles and the nearest to the original entrance. The name mocárabes means kinds of prefabricated plaster pieces which made up the vaulting. Wrecked in the explosion of 1590 this was replaced by a baroque ceiling of plaster. In the last century the southern end of the vault was taken down revealing the remains of the original, where one can see some of the polychroming and the spring of earlier work.

THE HALL OF THE ABENCERRAJES

We find this to the right as we pass anticlockwise through the colonnade. It is said that in Granada, myth and history are so intermixed that at times it is difficult to determine where one begins and the other ends. The name Abencerrajes belongs to a family of Granada of great political importance. Their rivals, the Zenetes, formed a conspiracy which implicated the Sultana in an amorous adventure, thus exciting the jealousy of the Sultan and leading to the massacre of thirty six Abencerrajes knights in this very hall, on the occasion of a party. This legend which was to inspire "The Last Abencerraje" by Chateaubriand, occurred during the reigns of a number of kings of Granada. Popular opinion has it that the red marks -iron oxide- on the bottom of the pool are the blood of the murdered knights.

This dodecagonal fountain is the central piece of the room, when filled and calm it reflects the magnificent mocarabes of the ceiling, with and eight-pointed star in the vaulting. From a seated position behind the fountain, before the Lions Fountain had the present spout, the view was a series of brilliant reflective planes and, at the far end through the Mirador of Lindaraja in the Hall of the Two Sisters one could see the old city and the sky. The original tiles in this room were taken to the Alcazar of Seville and replaced by the present ones in the sixteenth century.

In the south-east corner of the court is another exit leading to the gardens of the Partal and passing through a shell-domed tower. This is obviously another entrance to the Court of Lions coming from the Arrabal Gate near the Torre de los Picos which communicated with the approach road to the Generalife.

THE HALL OF KINGS

This occupies the whole east end of the Court of Lions. It is divided into five spaces; three of them lit by the access porticoes and separated by another two in the shade. In the springs of the vaulting of mocarabes there are twenty windows with plaster lattices. At the extreme ends are two alcoves with arches aligned along the axis of the room. From the southern alcove the rooms appear as a succession of areas of light and shade framed by plaster arches each different from the other.

This variety of decoration and alternating lights and shades results in this heavy decoration being pleasant to the eye without tiring in the way baroque decorative elements do when repeated over and again. The sensation of harmony with different elements is achieved in the ideal formula of modern decorators.

On the ceilings of the bigger alcoves there are paintings on vellum fixed to their wooden backing with paste and tiny bamboo pegs. This fixing system avoided damage which the rusting of iron nails would produce, and at the same time prevented the paintings from falling as the nails fixed in the wood loosened because of the differential thermal movement of the materials.

Veritable rivers of ink have been spent about the meaning of these paintings. Nowadays, however, there is little opposition to the demonstrated assertion of the French arabist Massignon. He destroyed the false argument which denies the eastern origin of these paintings founded on a supposed Koranic prohibition of representing living beings. The paintings of the Kings Hall are Moslem, even if influenced by western models, and it is generally believed that they were made in the late fourteenth or early fifteenth century. In fact in the Sura V, Aleya 92, the sacred book of the Mohammedan says: *"Oh, all those who believe! Verily, wine and the anzab, and the maisir and arrows (are) abominations and works by Shaitan; avoid them and probably you would be happy"*.

Thus all that is forbidden in relation to living beings are the anzab or idols which can be objects of adoration. This limitation is not exclusive to Islam; worshipping of idols is also prohibited in the Old Testament and in the Talmud. Also there are so many examples of living beings in Islamic art that just counting them would give the lie to this pretended prohibition.

The central alcove, given its privileged position, would have housed the Sultan and his intimates. Seated within, the perspective is of an oasis seen through a forest of palm trees with the Fountain of Lions at its centre. On the ceiling of this alcove ten persons are also painted who are traditionally thought to be the first ten kings of the dynasty. The silhouettes of hands and faces and the stars which divide the composition horizontally into two halves are painted on a golden background, all being reminiscent of early Byzantine panels.

The paintings in the other two alcoves share certain thematic elements. Two personages, one Christian and one Moslem, to judge by their arms and dress, perform a series of tests and trials, apparently for the favour of a Christian lady. All this terminates in the next alcove where the Moslem defeats his rival with a lance thrust before the pleading Christian dame who watches the trial from a tower.

THE HALL OF THE TWO SISTERS

Contrary to earlier opinion this is now recognised as the oldest of the rooms around the Court of Lions. As with all the other adjuncts of this court where we do not know the original name, the one given is merely descriptive. It is called **The Two Sisters** because of the two large Macael marble slabs in the centre of the room.

This room was used as the Hall of the Ambassadors by Muhammad V and replaced that built by his father for the same purpose in the Tower of Comares. It is decorated with a tiled dado decorated with the family coat of arms and metallic glazes, perhaps the most unusual in the whole of the Alhambra. Above this dado, written in Spanish cursive characters, is a beautiful qasida by Ibn Zamrak which covers the four walls. Starting from the left (facing the Fountain of the Lions) it describes the beauty of the room, comparing it to a beautiful garden. It also speaks of the marvellous vault of mocarabes which cover the room, a real masterpiece of over five thousand pieces.

The square floor of the eight-by-eight-metres room changes to an octagon in the upper part by means of squinches of mocarabes which support the eight-sided ceiling. Two windows are placed in each plane of the octagon and until 1590 they projected coloured light through stained glass. The aesthetic effect of the room is captured in a verse of the afore-mentioned qasida, in which it says:

"… in this the soul will find a beauteous dream"

Entering this hall from the Court of Lions we can see two narrow passages to left and right, as in the Hall of the Abencerrajes. The right-hand one provides stairs to the first floor and the left gives access to a toilet.

The Hall of the Two Sisters is paved with great slabs of marble and at each side of a small fountain there are the two largest ones which give the room its name.

Passing through the Hall of the Ajimeces with its windows to left and right and with a ceiling of mocarabes we find ourselves in the fabulous Mirador of Lindaraja.

MIRADOR OF LINDARAJA

The name seems to be derived from the Arabic "ain-dar-Aixa" (the eye of Aixa's House). It is possible that once he had finished the Court of the Lions and what remained to be done of the Court of Myrtles, Muhammad V once again used the Hall of Ambasadors and designated the Hall of the Two Sisters for use by the Sultana (dar-al-Malika) and the royal family as a residence. This arrangement is described by Hernando de Baeza, former interpreter to the court of Boabdil and then secretary of the Catholic Monarchs.

This gazebo, with window ledges at the original height, has on its north side a bealltiful "ajimez" which overlooks the Garden of Lindaraja. Before the Christian gallery which encloses the garden was built one could see the city over the walls, and then turning towards the Court of Lions from a seated position on the floor one saw the sky through the window over the arch at the entrance to the Hall of the Two Sisters.

Horizontally one saw the fountain of this room and the mirror of water of the Fountain of Lions. Crowning this gazebo which once housed the throne is a stained glass dome held in the finest of wooden tracery. This filled the room with multicoloured lights in olden times. Around the ajimez of the gazebo is a poem from which we quote this fragment:

> *"Certainly I am within this garden,*
> *an eye filled with joy,*
> *and the very apple of my eye is my Lord".*

Could this poetic image of the eye have something to do with the provisional throne and the name of the gazebo?

All the dados here in are formed of very smallest tiles or cut ceramics and the jambs of the arch which separate the gazebo from the Hall of the Ajimeces have ceramic inscriptions in black which refer to Muhammad V; they are cursive arabic script and seem to be inlaid in a white background.

THE PALACE OF CHARLES V

In the history of art there can be no building more vilified than the palace commissioned by Charles V next to the Alhambra (the royal palace of the Mussulmans).

It must be understood that, although he was unbeaten in his European campaigns and Paladin of the wars against Protestantism, Charles does not get a good press in European history and that all he did and all that he ordered built is mercilessly criticised. The many great things that were done in his reign go blindly and completely unrecognised.

Even worse, our own historians with a few exceptions have imbibed from these polluted sources which come from abroad. Thus we see, to show but one example, that don Francisco Pi Margall, without pausing to meditate on the architectural marvel he had before him, let his pen write, "*is this but a mass of stones distributed by neither intelligence nor sentiment, or is it simply the drafting of compass and rule?*".

Don Luis Hurtado de Mendoza had succeeded his father don Inigo when, in April 1562, he had news of the coming of the Emperor Charles V to Granada after his marriage to Isabel of Portugal in Seville that March. Bermúdez de Pedraza, the historian, tells us that the emperor did not intend to visit Granada, but did so at the request of certain personages and not solely because of the heat in Seville. They sang the praises of the city which thirty years earlier had been the pearl of the kingdom. Owing to its exotic past it was very attractive to the young king who had passed his early years in the monotony of the Low Countries.

On the twentieth of April the majordomo of the emperor arrived in Granada to organise the reception of his monarch, and finally on the fifth of June, Charles arrived in the company of the fair Isabel, one of the most beautiful women of her generation.

Seven years earlier an obscure reredos painter called Pedro Machuca had arrived, accompanying Jacobo Florentino. They came from Italy where Machuca had spent some years —it is not known how many—frequenting Italian circles and, perhaps in the company of the Florentines, he came into contact with the leading figures of the Arte Nuovo. Its influence can be seen in the palace that was to immortalise him as an architect.

Despite Antonio de Palomino describing him as "a follower of Rafael", it seems that Machuca never reached the grade of Master Architect, and consequently his work was confined to the precincts of the Alhambra by special jurisdiction. He also counted on the patronage of Luis Hurtado de Mendoza, Count of Tendilla and Governor of the Alhambra, whom he had served as squire in 1526 and to whom he was probably bound by mutual affection. It is known that his oldest son and daughter were called Luisa and Luis in honour of his noble patron.

Once Charles and his followers had arrived in Granada they were installed in some rooms built the year before, next to the upper part of the Baths of Comares and around the Court of Lindaraja and had access to the rest of the palace through the Hall of the Two Sisters and the Hall of Ambassadors.

The rooms later occupied by Washington Irving in 1829 were built for Isabel of Portugal, and an extra floor was added to the tower of Abu-l-Hayyay which was to be known as the "Peinador de la Reina". The court was housed in different parts of the city and the Queen, after moving her lodgings to the warden's apartments above the Mexuar, finally decided to move to the Convent of the Jeronimas which had recently been built. Until December when the royal couple left the city, this was the heart and brain of the Empire. By that time the empress was carrying the future Phillip II.

None of the more recent ancestors of Charles had had their own palace. With their evermoving courts they lodged in the houses of the nobility, in castles or monasteries.

Also, since the reign of the Catholic Monarchs and the early years of Charles' reign the colonial expansion looked towards Africa and the new lands of America. In the geopolitics of those times Granada had a privileged position as an inland city but not too far from the ports of embarkation for these continents. Because of his European education Charles could not live in the Nazari Palace, so he decided to build a palace on the Red Hill.

Pedro Machuca was commissioned to carry out the work with funds that Queen Juana of Castilla had destined, by order of her parents, for the repair of the old palaces, and 80,000 ducats which the emperor had received from the Moriscos of his kingdom.

The Morisco rebellion of 1568 put an end to the regular income to finance the works. After the 1550s the emperor's interest in his palace in the Alhambra was on the wane. Also his succesor, Philip II who was crowned king in 1556, was more interested in building the Escorial, leaving the Palace in the Alhambra in a secondary position. Successive delays, almost always due to a lack of funds, resulted in an unfinished palace up to the present day. It is considered to be the first non-religious renaissance building in Spain.

On the four exterior frontages one can see great differences between the two floors. The lower floor with the characteristic bugnato fiorentino (rustication), conserves the robustness of a medieval castle, while on the first floor (direct first by Luis Machuca and then by Juan de Orea) some "manerist" modifications by Juan de Herrera were introduced; for example, the illusion of walls of greater thickness produced by the round conical clerestory lights over the window.

On the western principal frontage the most notable features are the two winged, reclining women, softly carved in marble by the Flemish artist Antonio de Leval, which rest on the tympanum. He was also responsible for the cherubs above the tympana of the lateral doors, the medallions with Flemish warriors on them and the unfinished grey stone lions by the door of the south front.

Earl E. Rosenthal attributes the right hand relief (which represents the Battle of Pavia and everybody is left-handed) to this same Leval, though it is probably by Pedro Machuca. The left-hand relief (right-handed people) is by Juan de Orea. All the other reliefs are allusions to the Triumph of Peace, with angels burning flags and the tools of war in the desire for disarmament.

The upper part of the facade is neither as rich nor as interesting. it gives the impression that the original design was simplified to the minimum possible. Here we truly see the "compass and ruler" which Pi y Margall spoke of. Two medallions by Ocampo of the trials of Hercules are the only sculptural features of note on this upper body of the facade.

The south front, on the other hand, has the two bodies of the facade in elegant harmony, although the reliefs by Nicolao di Corte do not have the strength of those on the main front. The other two fronts, to the north and east, lack any features of interest.

The thirty-metre diameter central court, reached by climbing a few steps, is the master work in this palace. The lower part of this monumental ring of thirty two Tuscan-Doric columns of a smooth pudding stone (porphyry), are reminiscent of Bramante's San Pietro in Montorio, as if it were cast from the same mould as that building but in negative and on a much larger scale.

The solution of the architrave detail is completely original, creating a perfect balance between the forces and resistance of the components of which it is made up. This ring rests on a torus (the curved vault of the gallery)which carries perfectly the outward thrust of the stones like a continuous flying buttress, one part resting on the outer walls and the other on the ring-beam. When this wall is weakened by an opening, as occurs on the west side, the extra load is carried by a lower vault or some other means of buttressing.

The upper level of the court, with ionic columns of the same stone as those on the ground floor, was roofed in 1967 with a wooden "Artesonado". The deep box-moulding and radical beams could easily have been the work of Pedro Machuca himself. The same occurs with the staircase in the south-east corner leading to the Museo de Bellas Artes. With its bold curves this far surpasses the original seventeenth century one in the opposite corner, despite its modernity.

Attempts have been made to find precedents for the plan of this building. It has been written that it was inspired by the Palace of Caprarola by Vignola, but it must be remembered that that palace with its pentagonal plan and circular court, was built in 1546 while Machuca's project is almost twenty years earlier.

A special mention must be made of the so-called "Crypt" which was mentioned in relation to the Patio de los Arrayanes. This is to be found under the unfinished chapel in the north-east corner of the renaissance court. It is now reached by a stairway in the vestibule on the east side. It has an octagonal vault, almost flat in section and star-shaped in plan, and has no other form of support other than its own curvature. This can without any doubt be considered one of the works of genius of the Renaissance.

THE GENERALIFE

O f the pleasure gardens on the Cerro del Sol, the Generalife is the only one to survive to the present day.

It was an estate where the King of Granada retired, away from the preocupations of the Court. Its proximity to the Alhambra (apart from the advantage of one being close to the centre of government and thus being able to attend to urgent matters during the holidays) was also a sign of the richness of the owner: when transport was by mule or on foot a recreational estate so near to one's permanent residence was an indication that the owner was very rich.

The opulence of the owner was in direct relation to the proximity of his country house.

The meaning of the name "Generalife" is obscured in utter confusion. Yannat al´arif, so says Ibn Aljatib, means "principal 'huerta' " (small holding or country garden), according to Seco de Lucena. "Huerta of the Architect" say other authors without realising that "alarife" is a term which takes in many activities, apart from the one they mention.

Are any of the architects of the Alhambra known? Since the designers of the palaces have been conspicuously ignored in the inscription in the palaces, it seems stran-ge to dedicate the most important gardens in Granada, if not the whole kingdom, to one of them.

Because of the shortness of this work we will have to leave aside the many versions of the origin of the name Generalife, but we cannot resist giving at least one of our "crop": the function of the Generalife is that of a "carmen" (Granada house in the city, with a garden) the residence where the people of Granada went in the autumn, the most beautiful season in this region. At that time the temperature is mild with neither the oppressive heat of summer nor the dry cold of winter. There are still flowers in the gardens, blue skies and little rain most days.

If we accept that the root "Yannat" is prominent in the majority of the theories, why not Yannat al-jarif or "the autumn garden"?

The Generalife was given by the Reyes Católicos to the 'comendador' (Warden) Hinestrosa. By a series of inheritances and marriages, etc. it came into the hands of the Granada Venegas family, thence finally to the Marqueses of Campotejar who were related to the Grimaldi-Palavicini from Milan. Following a long court case in which the State claimed ownership of the Generalife, the case was found in favour of the owners, who ceded the Palace to the Spanish State without cost, in 1921. For this act of generosity Alfonso XIII created the title of Marques del Generalife.

All that remains of the original gardens are the terraces where they were planted. These workings reached to the top of the mount so that, from the top, one saw them as one entity down to the foot of the hill, with the variety of colours which the flowers and fruit trees imprinted on each of the steps. The present gardens have nothing in common with Medieval Gardens where flowers and fruits were mixed heterogeneously. In the present gardens only the senses of smell and sight are played upon. In the Mussulman garden one enjoyed the sight of the flowers, their perfume, the sound of water and the taste of the fruit eaten as one passed under the trees. This was a "huerta", a word difficult to translate into many languages, from the Latin 'hortus' and which was the common description of what today we call "jardín" or garden.

Any panoramic view from the Alhambra alone explains the reasons that promted its founder, the Al-Ahmar, to choose these hills for his palaces. They only lacked water to be perfect. The river Darro was diverted for 18 kms. to convert this wasteland into an oasis, the Paradise promised on Earth. Dams, channels, cisterns, siphons, ponds, right up to sand filters, all the mastery of Arab engineering, in short, was put to a human dimension.

Agriculture had been born in the East, the garden and the myth of the Earthly Paradise, idealized in the traditions and trnasmitted by the most ancient cultures which man has reported.

It would be difficult to imagine such irrigation in the Rhine, while the Euphrates, the Tigris and the Nile fertilize the deserts in this way. The Arabs, eager nomads and heirs of these traditions, mastered as no-one else, the physical laws that applied to water to confer the lifegiving force, symbolic of life, a subtle and mysterious nature that inpregnates these Gardens and Palaces with magic. Water was always the principal problem but also the first to be solved, to such a point, that its abundance determined the accessions during the successive invasions and re-population. Without water, neither Granada nor the Alhambra would be where they are.

To describe the Generalife, as it is known, it is necessary to refer to the Agriculture and Gardening treaty of Ibn Luyun, who listed the conditions, at the beginnung of the XIV century, that should to fulfil a property of this type:

"A small hill must be chosen to site a house among gardens so that it facilitates observation and guarding. The building should face south as too should the entrance to the property. The pond or well should be on higher ground, or better still, from the well, water channels run under the shades of the trees. All around there massive trees should be planted that are always green and all other kinds of plants that gladden the sight and, somewhat more separated, various varieties of flowers and other perrenial trees. A fence of vines should surround the garden and, in the center, the grapevines should shade the roads that straddle the paths.

A pavilion should be raised in the center for rest hours, surrounded by climbing rosebushes, myrtles and other varieties of flowers that beautify a garden. It should be long and wide so that it does not tire the eye while gazing upon it. In the lower part, a room should be built for the guests of the propietor. There should be a pond, hidden among the trees so that it cannot be seen from a distance. It is also convenient to build a dovecot and a small habitable tower, The house must have tow doors, so that remains more protected and it will be more restful for those that inhabit it."

All these conditions are found in what remains of the much-altered residence around the so called Patio de laAcequia (Court of the Canal or reservoir). The 'canal', which runs North-South along the spine of the court has, since the romantic period, two rows of spouts which, form water arches cascading into the canal in the Italianate manner. In this way the mirror effect which the pond had in the time of the Nazaries is broken and the air is filled with obsessive noise made as the fountains hit the surface of the water.

In the original design the water entered from the two fountains at the ends of the pool, forming a pleasant murmur, like calming music which does not interfere with one's thoughts.

In the time of the Reyes Catolicos some arches were opened in the western wall of the court, and its height was lowered. In the Islamic period there was only one opening in the wall, the pavillion at the middle.

The North end, the best preserved, is fronted by an arcade of round-headed arches. The centre one greater in height. These three arches of similar design are the entrance to a transverse space, covered with a wooden "lazo" ceiling. .The presence of a poem dates this building to the year 1319.

Translated by David H. Beaman

Edición y realización: Juan Agustín Núñez Guarde. EDILUX.
Fotografía: Miguel Román Vega y Juan Agustín Núñez.
Maquetación del texto: Germán Madinabeitia.
ISBN-84-87282-51-2 D.L. GR-1.925-89.
Encuardernación: Hnos Olmedo.

Texto: Aurelio Cid Acedo
Dibujos: Javier Bosch y José M. Medina.
Planos infográficos :Manuel Castillo
Impresión: Al sur, Copartgraf y Mateu Cromo.
Filmación: Franacolor.   Made in Spain

Generalife

Carlos V

Pags. 60-64: **Palacio de Carlos V, detalles** — Palace of Charles the V, details — Palace de Charles V, détailles — Palast von Karl V, Details — Palazzo di Carolo V, particolari

Court of arms of the Catholic Kings.

CRISTIAN GRANADA

Granada, "a delight to the eye and a comfort to the soul"—was so described by an Arab poet, before it passed into the hands of the Christians. Long before being reconquered in 1492, it was coveted for its unequalled natural beauty, for the magnificence of its palaces, and for its impressive fortress of the Alhambra.

Much before 1492 and the fall of the city and its occupation by the Christians, they were bent upon possessing rather than destroying Granada. In order to understand the history of this city, (both Moslem and Christian), we must keep in mind the eight centuries of strife between them. This yearning for possession is born of a desire to make this city a historic symbol, and because of this, it created a compendium of great Renaissance and Baroque works of art, that continue the fame and beauty attained during the Moslem Middle Ages.

To understand the reality of this city we must realize that Christian Granada is a symbiosis of Moorish and Christian (Morisco and Mudejar) cultures. In most cases the greatest achievements of the new image of the city, created in the Renaissance and Baroque periods and later in the Romantic period of the XIX century, arise from the rich inheritance of the Nazarite period.

It is a pity that the twentieth century city has not known, for the most part, how to make urban renewal compatible with modernization and respect for the past. The towers of the Alhambra, high above the city, tell us part of the tale. The rest is told by the towers and cupola of the Cathedral, the Renaissance and Baroque churches and the convents of the Albaycin. All this is surrounded by the luxuriant beauty of the vega (the valley) and the massive and impressive Sierra Nevada with its frosty peaks of Mulhacen and Veleta.

How shall we approach Christian Granada? Shall we follow the steps of the protagonists: the conquerers, the so called—Cotholic Monarchs—, Carlos V, or their heirs and governors? Better yet: let's visit the monuments which have beautified and universalized Granada.

PLANO DE GRANADA
MONUMENTAL

SACROMONTE

MONUMENTOS

1- CARTUJA
2- HOSPITAL REAL
3- PUERTA MONAITA
4- ARCO DE LAS PESAS
5- PALACIO DALAHORRA
6- STA. ISABEL LA REAL
7- SAN MIGUEL BAJO
8- PUERTA ELVIRA
9- SAN CRISTOBAL
10- EL SALVADOR
11- SAN NICOLAS
12- PALACIO DE LOS CORDOVA
13- ABADIA DEL SACROMONTE
14- CASA DE CASTRIL
15- SAN PEDRO Y SAN PABLO
16- STA. ANA
17- AUDIENCIA - CHANCILLERIA
18- GENERALIFE
19- ALHAMBRA
20- CARMEN DE LOS MARTIRES
21- TORRES BERMEJAS
22- SAN CECILIO

23- CASA DE LOS TIROS
24- CASA DE LOS GIRONES
25- SANTO DOMINGO
26- SANTIAGO
27- SAN MATIAS
28- BASILICA DE N.ª S.ª DE LAS ANGUSTIAS
29- CORRAL DEL CARBON
30- LA ALCAICERIA
31- ARZOBISPADO
32- PALACIO DE LA MADRAZA
33- CATEDRAL
34- UNIVERSIDAD
35- COLEGIATA SAN JUSTO Y PASTOR
36- SAN JUAN DE DIOS
37- SAN JERONIMO

MUSEOS

A- MUSEO ARQUEOLOGICO PROVINCIAL
B- MUSEO DE BELLAS ARTES Y MUSULMAN
C- MUSEO Y CARMEN DE LA FUNDACION RODRIGUEZ ACOSTA
D- MUSEO DE HISTORIA DE GRANADA

a MURCIA y ALMERIA

C. DE LA ALBERZANA

BLANQUEO NUEVO
BLANQUEO VIEJO

C. DE SAN LUIS

C. PAGES

C. ALMONA

C. PANADEROS

PL. AITAR

C. SAN NICOLAS
PL. SAN NICOLAS
CAMINO NUEVO DE SAN NICOLAS

C. SAN LUIS

C. SAN CRISTOBAL

CENICEROS

CUESTA DE LA ALHACABA

CALLEJON DE LAS MINAS
CUESTA DE MARIA
LA MIEL

ALMIRANTE

C. DE LA TIÑA

C. DE

C. DE OIDORES

C. SAN JO

PL. SAN MIGUEL BAJO
C. DEL GALLO

C. DEL ZENETE

CARRIL DE LA LONA

C. DEL MOLINO DE LA
CUESTA BETETA

CARRETERA DE MURCIA

C. DEL CAMINO DE SAN ANTONIO

C. CUESTA SAN ANTONIO

CRISTO DE LA YEDRA

CARRETERA DE ALFACAR

C. REAL DE CARTUJA

AV. DE MURCIA

C. DEL CRISTO DE LA YEDRA
C. DEL AGUA
C. DE LA PARRA ALTA
C. NUEVA
PL. DE LA CRUZ

C. ACERA DE SAN ILDEFONSO

PL. DE LA MERCED

PL. DEL TRIUNFO

C. DE ELVIRA

PASEO DEL TRIUNFO

C. DEL HOSPITAL

AV. DE PULIANAS

C. ANCHA DE CAPUCHINOS

C. DE LA DIVINA PASTORA

GRAN VIA DE COLON

PL. DE SAN ISIDRO

a MADRID y JAEN

AV. DE MADRID

AV. DE LA CONSTITUCION

C. SAN JUAN DE DIOS

C. NATALIO RIVAS
C. NUEVA DEL STMO.
CARDENAL MENDOZA
C. LAVADERO DE LA CRUZ

C. SANTA PAULA
C. DE LOS ARANDAS
MARQUES DE FALCES

C. MANO DEL HIERRO

C. SAN JERONIMO
C. DE LOS COLEGIOS

PL. UNIVERSIDAD

C. CANASTEROS

C. ALMONAR
C. VENTANILLA

C. DE LA FUENTENUEVA

C. RECTOR LOPEZ ARGUETA

AV. DE DOCTOR OLORIZ

a MALAGA y SEVILLA

C. CUENCA
C. DEL GRAN CAPITAN
C. DE TRIANA
C. MARQUES DE FALCES

RIO DARRO

CTA. DEL CHAPIZ

12

CUESTA DE LA VICTORIA

C. DE GUMIEL

C. HORNO DEL ORO

C. DEL CANDIL

PASEO DE LOS TRISTES

CUESTA DEL STMO.

18

CUESTA DE LOS CHINOS

14A 15

C. ZAFRA

C. CONCEPCION

C. CARNERO

RIO DARRO

CARRERA DEL DARRO

19

B

16

C. SAN

GREGORIO

17 PL. DE SANTA ANA

CUESTA GOMEREZ

PL. NUEVA

C. CALDERERIA NUEVA

C. REYES CATOLICOS

C. JOAQUIN COSTA

C. ABENHAMAR

PL. DE ISABEL LA CATOLICA

D

29

VIA DE COLON

C. SAN AGUSTIN

32

C. ZACATIN

C. CARCEL BAJA

33

30

31

PL. DE LAS PASIEGAS

PL. DE LA ROMANILLA

PL. BIBRAMBLA

C. SALAMANCA

C. PESCADERIA

BOTEROS

C. DE MESONES

PUERTA REAL

DE LA DUQUESA

PL. TRINIDAD

C. DE LA ALHONDIGA

C. DE LAS TABLAS

C. RECOGIDAS

C. DE PUENTEZUELAS

C. DE AGRELA

C. DE LA VERONICA DE LA MAGDALENA

23 D

C. PAVANERAS

24

25

C. SAN MATIAS

27

PL. DEL CARMEN

C. REYES CATOLICOS

C. DE NAVAS

C. ANGEL GANIVET

PL. MARIANA PINEDA

PL. CAMPILLO BAJO

PL BIBATAUBIN

21

C. DEL AIRE

PUERTA SOL

DAMASQUEROS

CUESTA REAL

COCHERAS

C. DEL HUERTO

PL. CAMPO DEL PRINCIPE

C

22

C. ANTEQUERUELA BAJA

AUDITORIO MANUEL DE FALLA

CAMINO NUEVO DEL CEMENTERIO

20

CUESTA DEL CAIDERO

C. DE BELEN

C. MOLINOS

C. DE SANTIAGO

26

C. PACO SECO DE LUCENA

C. ENRIQUETA

C. SAN JACINTO

C. SAN PEDRO MARTIR

28

CARRERA DEL GENIL

ACERA DEL DARRO

PASEO DE LA BOMBA

a SIERRA NEVADA

RIO GENIL

PASEO DEL SALON

C. SAN ISIDRO

C. SAN ANTON

C. NUEVA DE SAN ANTON

C. ALHAMAR

RIO GENIL

a MOTRIL Y ALMERIA

PASEO DEL VIOLON

LA CAPILLA REAL

THE RENAISSANCE AND THE BAROQUE PERIOD

Triumphant with the conquest of Granada, Fernando and Isabel soon organized endowments for the creation of monuments that will make apparent to all, the true historical importance of their feat, not only for the city of Granada but for all the nation. While planning the construction of a Cathedral over the Major Mosque of the city they first established a provisional one in the Mosque of the Alhambra on May 21, 1492. By 1501 the Catholic Monarchs had decreed that all the properties and patrimony of all the mosques of Granada should be endowed to the yet to be built Cathedral .

But by far the greatest legacy left to the city by the Catholic Monarchs was the decision to build a chapel in the city to be known as "de los Reyes" (of the Monarchs), that was to be their final resting place. Desirous of making this city the symbol of their greatest political dreams, they decreed in Medina del Campo on September 13, 1504 that in the new Cathedral a chapel should be built "at the right hand of the Main Chapel and patronized by SS John the Baptist and John the Evangelist. It was established that in perpetuity this chapel would be attended by thirteen chaplains who would offer three daily masses for their souls and those of their ancestors and heirs. That three anniversary masses would be celebrated after their demise and on all All Saints Day. They also decreed that in this chapel should be placed the Blessed Sacrament, and before it, day and night, perpetually, a six pound candle should be lit and two oil lamps should be placed specifically for the devotion to the Sacrament.

After founding the Chapel, they ordered

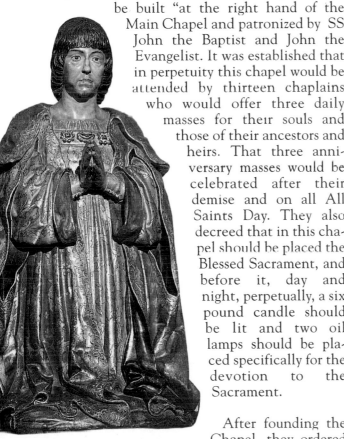

Statues of the Catholic Quings praying.
Left: The Grill of master Bartolomé.

in their testaments, that should they die before the completion of the Chapel, they should be taken to the monastery of San Francisco in the Alhambra to be interred until the Royal Chapel should be ready to receive them. Isabel died in 1504 and Fernando in 1516 but it was not until the 10th of November of 1521 that the conquerers of Granada were taken to their final resting place, in a solemn procession from the Alhambra to the newly consecrated Chapel.

The key to an era, the design and building of the Royal Chapel, were commissioned to Enrique Egas, the major architect of the Catholic Monarchs, on the 30th of October 1506. His design of great simplicity and austerity was probably made following the desires of Cardenal Cisneros and the Queen herself. But this simplicity was later to displease the representative of the Monarch and Carlos V, himself, who considered that the glory of his grandparents merited a more grandiose treatment.

The Chapel, of Latin Cross design, with elevated choir, is a fine example of Isabelline Gothic. The style of the Chapel and its proportions, the cresting on its outer walls, Isabel's and Fernando's shields and initials, which are found on the southern and only exterior facade of the building, are clear examples of late Gothic with early indications of Renaissance style. All this is a clear manifestation of the modernity of the Catholic Monarchs and their heirs.

Its **original main entrance**, on the north side, and inside the Cathedral is an excellent example of Ogival art with many royal crests, initials with crowned yoke and arrows and a dedication that reads "Laudet eam opera eius" (May their works be praised). It is formed by a semi-circular ornamental arch on whose sides stand the images of the SS John the Baptist and Evangelist and heralds carrying staffs which seems to convert the

5

Mausoleum of Felipe el Hermoso (Philip the Handsome) and Johanna the Mad by Bartolomé Ordóñez.
Sceptre of Queen Isabel.

openinging in a triumphal arch. It is believed that Enrique Egas directed the work

The entrance at the foot of the Chapel is of interest as it connects with the ancient Nazarite Mesquita, used as a cathedral before the construction of the modern one. Today it connects with the baroque church of El Sagrario. Of special value, flanking the doorway are the lovely stone polychromed figures of St. Peter and St. Paul who symbolically seem to be guarding the church .

The third entrance opened in the exterior wall in 1527, some years after the completion of the chapel, is of Plateresque style and was probably designed by Juan García de Praves. Only the upper part remains as originally designed. The Portal and the adjacent Lonja contrast with the Gothic design and decoration of the rest of the façade; the repetition of the Royal initials in the ornamental stone filigree balustrades, the gargoyles and the miniature pinnacles with their crockets. The lower half of the doorway is a poor XVII century restoration, but

the imperial seal with its two-headed eagle in the center continues to symbolize the royal foundation of this building. Each detail seems to call out the courtly character of this place—the essence of the new city—aulic Christian constructions in the heart of Moslem Granada, surrounded by the Mesquita, Madraza, Fonde and commercial center.

The interior of the monument, in accord with its funerary character, is a private and public place. Its private and solemn character is accentuated by its proportions, subdued lighting, the chromatic tones of the whole and originally by the gilded Gothic letters on its walls and its polychromed royal crests.

Round the walls runs an inscription in gilded Gothic characters stating that the Catholic Monarchs had conquered Granada and converted it to their faith, that they had built chur-

Mausoleum of Felipe el Hermoso (Philip the Handsome) and Johanna the Mad by Bartolomé Ordóñez

ches, monasteries and hospitals and that they had expelled the Moors.

In the geometric center of the transept are the Royal tombs with their effigies in Carrara marble made by the Italian sculptor Domenico Alexandro Fancelli. This harmonious but monumental work was commissioned by the Emperor Carlos V. in honour of his grandparents. It contrasts greatly with the simple tomb that Isabel had envisaged, as can be seen below in the crypt.

LA REJA (IRON GRILL)

The magnificent Reja, the work of Master Bartolome in 1520, is one of the finest grill works in all of Spain, and a most singular chapter in Spanish Renaissance art. The light at dusk, in the silent temple seems to set the polychromed and gilded part of the grill aflame, stretching its transparent web across the nave before the transept and is for this reason farther forward than the usual chancel screen. The filtered light rests upon the solemn tombs and on the sculptured elements of the great retablo of Felipe de Vigarni. Except for the open central panel the reja separates the royal sepulchral monument from the nave. In it all the fantasies of Plateresque art are expressed.

Divided in three storeys, the lowest has six Corinthian columns with Plateresque adornments supporting the royal arms, angels, intertwined foliage, and on the columns are figures of the apostles on pedestals and crowned with Gothic canopies, motif which also decorates the third level. Above this, rises the masterpiece of sculpture in iron, ten episodes from the life of Christ, the martydoms of SS John the Baptist and Evangelist and towering above all, in the center, the Crucifixion. Part of the reja's magnificence is most certainly due to the proximity of vertical and horizontal straight lines and to the intricate ornamental patterns in iron.

THE TOMB AND THE RETABLO

Above the crypt are the two impressive catafalques in marble. The sepulchral monuments of the Catholic Monarchs, to the right, are the

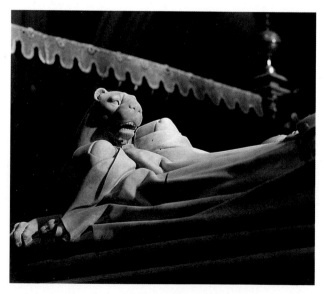

Details of the Mausoleum of Phillip and Johanna

work of the Italian Fancelli. They were carved in Genoa, finished in 1517 in Granada and placed in 1522. Of Carrara marble of exceptional quality and tone the tomb of the Catholic Monarchs is according to Bertaux *"the union of Florentine grace and Spanish grandeur"*. On the top the monument are the recumbent figures with serene profiles slightly turned away from one another; Isabel is wearing a tunic and cloak and hanging from a chain a medallion of the Order of Santiago. Fernando is wearing a full suit of armour, partially covered with a cloak and about his neck a medallon with a relief of Saint George. The monument has a quadrangular base with inclined sides decorated with figures of the apostles and at the four corners are fantastical griffins with lion claws and eagle wings.

Among the Greeks the griffins were thought to be guardian monsters who protected treasures while the Christians considered them to be cruel and evil forces. Above each griffin is a saint—four guardians of the Church—St. Agustine, St. Jerome, St. Ambroise and St. Gregory—who probably represented the triumph of Christianity over paganism. The theme is treated repeatedly throughout the sculpture with allegories of Pegasus, Centurions, Phoenix, skulls, and these symbols combined with political ones such as the pomegranate, lion, castle, and yoke and arrow.

On each side of the lower level we have representations of the Resurrection, the

Baptism of Christ, Saint George and Saint James. On three sides of the upper level are royal seals carried by angels and on the fourth side, at their feet, is an inscription that boasts that Fernando and Isabel had expelled the Moors from Granada. At the foot of each figure and as though guarding their eternal sleep are a lion and a lioness. In conclusion, it was with this sepulchre that a long period of change ends and a modern era begins. The renaissance tomb under the dome of a Gothic chapel is the happy evidence of the political cultural moment.

On the left is the tomb of Juana la Loca and her husband Felipe the Fair. The work was commissioned to Bartolme Ordoñez by Carlos V. in 1519. The sculptor, clearly influenced by Michelangelo, is considered one of the four greatest artists of the Spanish Renaissance. Most of his work was done in Italy and for Italy. While working on this sepulchre, at Carrara, he died before it was completed.

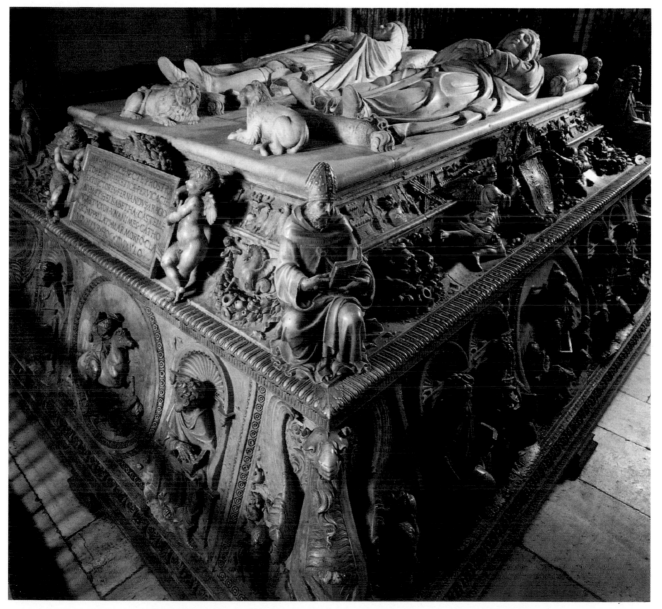

Crown of Queen Isabel and Mausoleum of the Queens by Domenico Fancelli.

Central detail of the Grill. Master Bartolomé de Jaén. Down: Façade of the Royal Chapel.

Granada by Buckmall Estcourt.

The work of this colleague of Diego de Siloe is similar in style to Fancelli's as is confirmed by the great sculptural monument. In contrast to the serenity of the figures of the Catholic Monarchs, Ordoñez bestows upon his work qualities of greater plastic movement and more daring contrasts. This funerary monument has high vertical walls upon which rests a tomb on which lie the recumbant figures. The Monarchs richly attired, he with a sword and she with a scepter, have idealized profiles. The Queen's countenance has especially inspired poets over the centuries as in the case of Federico García Lorca who praises her beauty in "Elegy to Juana la Loca". On the lower part of the base are circular reliefs depicting scenes related to the life of Christ and twelve niches separated by balustered columns in which are placed the seven virtues and five allegories. Of special note are Fortitude, Temperance, Theology and Mathematics. On the high corners, beside the King he has finished a sculpture of St. Andrew and left St. Michael roughly prepared. Beside the Queen are the two Johns. On the lower part are mythical figures and the symbols of the Monarchs, a chain for the Duchy of Burgundy and the yoke and arrows and

Jewel box-reliquary from Q'ueen Isabel.

granada (Pomegrenate) for the heirs of the Catholic Monarchs. On the side of the feet is a lovely XVIII century epitaph supported by angels that expounds the virtues of this King and Queen and explains that they are the parents of the Emperor Carlos V. who ordered the construction of this monument.

Mausoleum of the Catholic Quings. Domenico Fancelli.

Because this tomb is higher than the other it gives an unbalanced front view. Only a lateral view from the right side of the transept allows us to view both works jointly.

Beneath these sepulchres is the burial crypt under an austere vault of stone. The lead caskets are placed with awesome simplicity on plain slabs of quarry stone. Seeing this simplicity one understands the original intention and request made by Queen Isabel in the second clause of her testament. She states therein that she wishes to be buried with the greatest simplicity and without pomp and that all that would have been spent on such ceremonies be given to the poor.

In the center of the crypt today are, the caskets with the remains of Queen Isabel and of King Fernando. At the sides are those of Queen Juana la Loca and King Felipe the Fair and a small coffin which contains the remains of Prince Miguel, a grandchild of the Catholic Monarchs and son of Isabel, the oldest daughter of the Monarchs, and the King of Portugal. Because of the unexpected death of this child the crown of Aragon and Castilla passed into the hands of prince Carlos, son of Juana and Felipe. The first wife of king Herry the VIII, Catherine of Aragón, was also the daughter of these kings. Other members of the Royal family were buried here until 1574 when they were all transferred to El Escorial, which replaced Granada as the site of the Royal Pantheon.

Facing the tombs is a wide marble stairway flanked by ornate marble han-

Detail of the Mausoleum. Fancelli.

drails carved with foliage and grotesque figures, the creation of the Italian, Francisco Florentin. Dominating all of the chapel and especially the presbytery, over the main altar and at the head of the stairs, is the great retablo of Felipe de Vigarni. The work is one of the first in Plateresque style in Spain. Its architectural and decorative format is noteworthy but most outstanding is the sculptural work. The gilding of the patrons, Saint John the Baptist and the Evangelist, is excellent and also noteworthy is the Adoration of the Magi, in the center and at bench height, is the resemblance of the youngest king to Carlos V.

At the sides of the retablo are the Catholic Monarchs orantes, (praying) an idealized though excellent work of Diego de Siloe. Fernando is placed next to the panel of the surrender of Granada with King Boabdil handing over the keys of the city to the Catholic Monarchs and Isabel next to the relief, on the right, which shows the conversion of the Moors. The retablo is the backcloth that closes all of this iconographic program of glorification and commemoration of the people and events that protagonized the first glorious days of modern Christian Granada. Only the work of the great Spanish Renaissance sculptor and artist Alonso de

Saint John the Evangelist by Bartolomé Ordoñez.

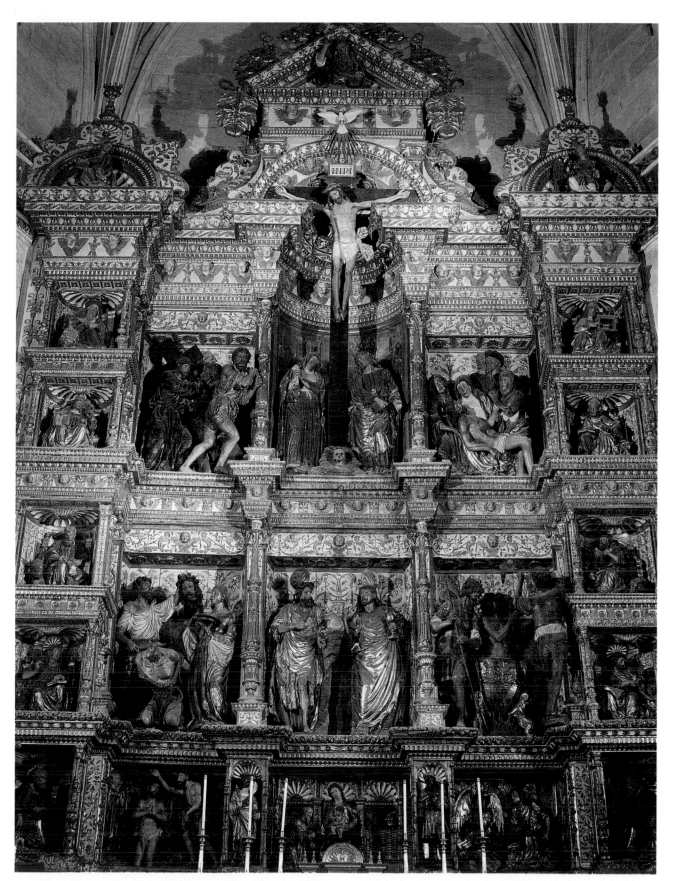

Decoratión of the high Altar, work of the sculptor Felipe de Vigarny, (1520-1522), with scenes of the Passion of Christ in the top part with reffrence to ss. John the Baptist and Evangelist in the central part. The adoration of the monarchs is at the botton.

Berruguete is missing. There are critics who, however, find evidence of his style in the expressive and overwhelming scenes of the Martydom of Saint John and Christ carrying the Cross on the left side of the retablo, which is totally different from all the work on the right side.

OTHER RETABLOS AND THE SACRISTY MUSEUM

Two magnificent retablos were added at the transept during the baroque period in which are incorporated cupboards and reliquaries. The many carvings and paintings are the work of Alonso de Mena and were completed in

1632. There is an important number of paintings on wood and relics in the interior, as well as jewels which belonged to the Catholic Monarchs who donated them to this Chapel.

On these retablos and on its benches, are the carved portraits of the Monarchs, D. Felipe, Dona Juana, Carlos V, the empress Isabel, Felipe IV and his wife Isabel de Borbon. The richness of the gilded and polychromed Baroque work of these retablos, contrasts greatly with the marble tombs and the copy of the world famous painting of Rogier van der Weyden, the Descent from the Cross which is in the Prado Museum.

On the other side of the transept is the Isabelline entrance of the sacristy, today the Treasury of the Chapel. Inside is a museum of works of arts and mementos of great artistic and historic value. Historically of great significance are the crown and scepter of the Queen and the florentine sword of King Fernando. carrried each year on the second day of January, through the streets of Granada to commemorate the surrender of the city by the Moors.

First known portrait-sculpture of Charles V.
Sword of D. Fernando with a hilt of gold.
Left: Details of the High Altar.

In addition to these important treasures are banners, pennants, standards and flags that belonged to the Castillian armies during the War of Granada. We can also see chalices and vestments embroidered in gold, that were also donated by the Catholic Monarchs for their Chapel . The Queen's mirror, converted into a monstrance, and then returned to its original state is also here.

There are numerous works of the Flemish school and others by Spanish and Italian masters. Of the exhibited works—outstanding among the best—is a set of two panels, the Pieta and the Nativity, of a triptych by the great Flemish master Van der Weyden. The third section, the Resurrection, is in the New York Metropolitan Museum. In this great work of Marian theme the artist offers the three most crucial moments in the life of the Virgin with relation to Jesus Christ: Birth, Death and Resurrection. After his experience as a sculptor, Van der Weyden, inspired by his masters the Van Eycks, knew how to transmit in his paintings all of the unrestrained power of the new approach to interpreting art. In this work, especially in the Pieta, he offers us his most categorically vigorous and creative style. His forceful palette dramatically emphasizes the clear diagonal between the body of Christ upon the black cloak of the Virgin accentuating the tragic union of the two heads. The background of this painting, differs from the triptych of the same theme that is in the Prado Museum in Madrid.

After the last restoration the magnificent Triptyck of the Passion by Diereick Bouts pre-

Detail of the Descent by Dierick Bouts

sides over the actual museum of the Sacristy . This belonged to Queen Isabel and it is, without a doubt, the most treasured and beautiful work of all of the Chapel. The Descent from the Cross, perfection of colour and sensibility in its entirely, is flanked on the right by the Crucifixion and on the left by the Resurrection. This work and the benches, by Pedro Machuca and Florentin, were all carefully restored and placed here in 1945 and 1993.

The contemplation of these outstanding works requires time and concentration. The pleasure of the aesthetic works combined with the historic significance of this chapel has attracted travellers from all over the world. Visitors, who come to appreciate this Granada of the Catholic Monarchs, this fusion and contrast of two cultures: the Alhambra with its Royal Palaces and this sepulchral chapel, treasury and museum. Here in the intimacy of this chapel our imaginations take flight and we clearly perceive the splendour of renaissance Granada with relation to Europe and America. Certainly, we should recall here that these Monarchs, Fernando and Isabel, together with Christopher Colombus, began in this city one of man's most important exploits: the discovery of America.

Velázquez (Ca. 1.630)

The Descent by Dierick Bouts.

17

Detail of the portrait of Crist by Dierk Baouts (1420-1475)

Detail of the left panel of the triptych of the altarpiece of the holy cross.

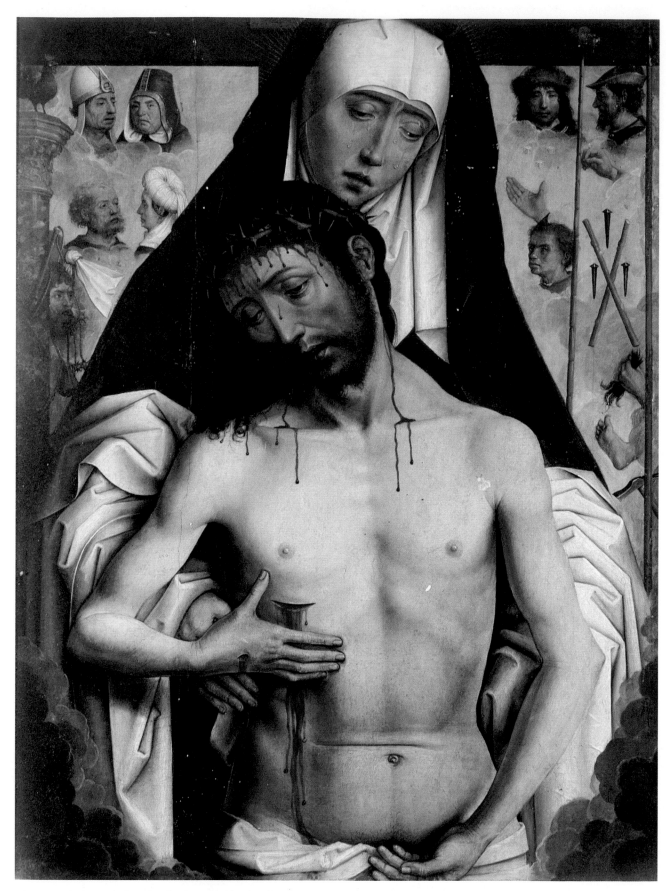

The Piety and Christ. Work attributed to Hans Memling (1455-1495). Museum of the Sacristy. Royal Chapel.

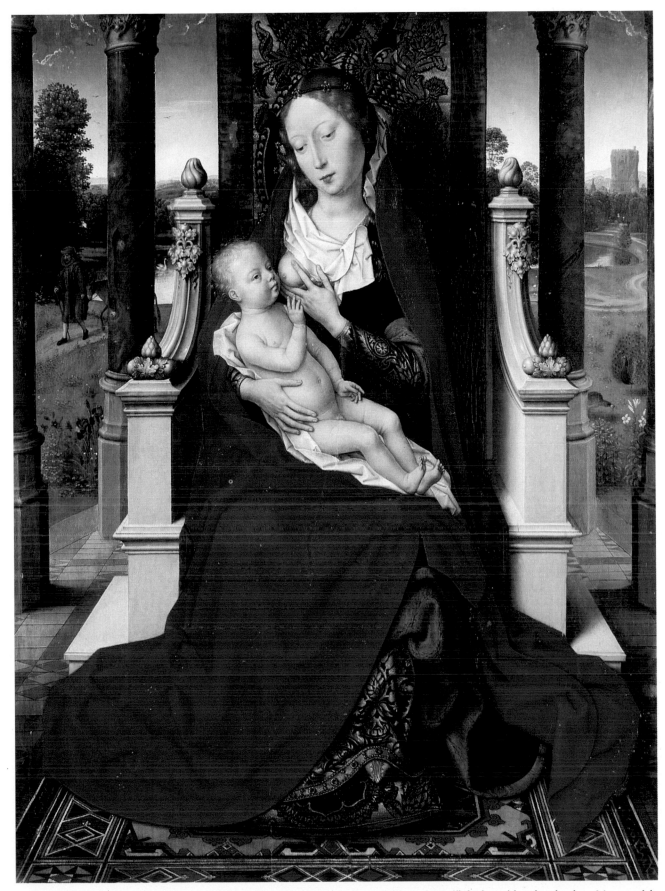

Virgin and Child painting on wood by master Hans Memling. The richness of colour and delicate design fill this beautiful work with valour. Museum of the Sacristy. Royal Chapel.

LA CATEDRAL

THE CATHEDRAL

This part of the city, called by the Moslems "of Hara Alchama" (of the Major Mosque) was chosen by the Catholic Monarchs to build the first and most important Christian temples. First, the Mezquita (today the Sagrario) was consecrated and dedicated to Our Lady of O. Later, on its north side the construction of the actual Cathedral was planned and next to it, as we have already seen, the Royal Chapel. Thus, this place which has been the heart of Moslem life, became the hub of the new Christian city.

The nearby Madraza (Moslem religious school and University) was founded in about 1349 by King Yusuf I and was, one of the most important buildings of the Nasarite city. After the Christian conquest the Catholic Monarchs granted the building to the city, and from 1500 to 1851 it was the Town Hall. Today this building has a lovely XVIII century facade and a superb mudejar hall. The Plaza de Bibrambla, (expanded between 1516 and 1519), the walls of the city and the Alcaiceria (silk bazaar), bordered this district on the west. Parallel to the right bank of the River Darro, was the Zacatin, the most important street in the city. Modern XX century urban renewal on the north side and the opening of the Gran Via, slowly transformed this medieval quarter of narrow and intercrossed streets. In Nazarite times it was, one of the most populated parts of the city.

In this district, close to the Mezquita, as we have said, the construction of the new Cathedral was planned. A Gothic design was most definitely planned, inspired by the Cathedral of Toledo, when Enrique Egas was commissioned in 1518 to take charge of the floor plan. This district was clearly intended to be Gothic as can be seen in the Royal Chapel and in the old Lonja (Exchange) building, which were undertaken in the same year, intermixing Gothic, Mudejar and Plateresque styles. However, once the foundations were laid for the Cathedral a Renaissance style was chosen, making it the first in Spain in the new style.

From the 25th of March 1523, when the first stone was placed, until 1528 Enrique Egas and Sebastian de Alcantara directed the construc-

Gate of Perdon by Diego de Siloé.
Left interior view of the Cathedral from the main Chapel.

23

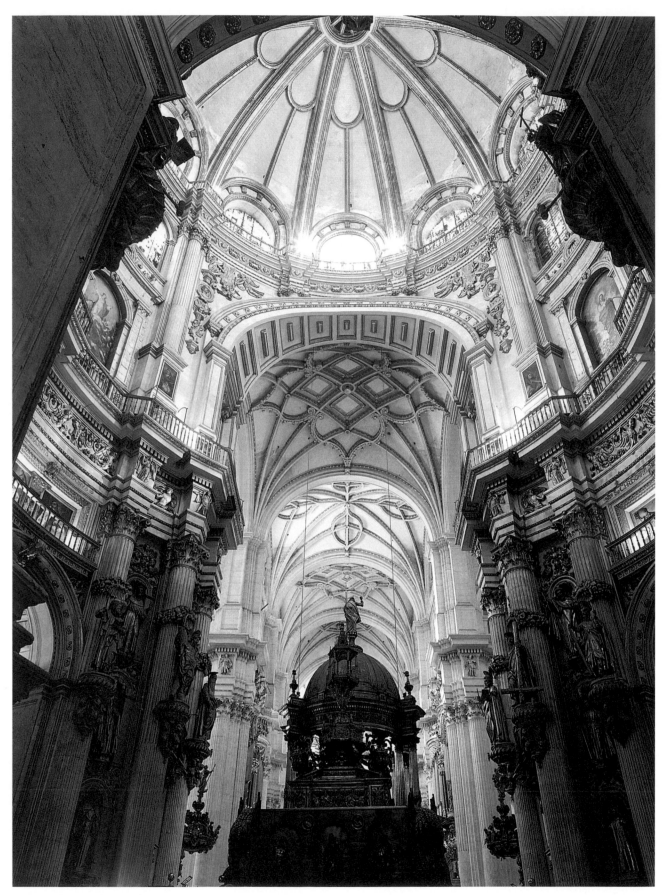

Interior of the Cathedral from the Ambulatory.

Main Chapel.

tion of the Gothic Cathedral. At this time Egas was relieved of his post. It appears that the new artistic trends apparent in the city, where much new construction was underway, was soon to affect the style of the new Cathedral. At that time Jacobo Florentino was working on the church-monastery of San Jeronimo and Pedro Machuca on the palace of Carlos V in the Alhambra. These buildings along with the decoration of the Royal Chapel, in the new Renaissance style, were receiving much enthusiastic interest.

Diego de Siloe, from Burgos, had come to Granada to work on the church of San Jeronimo, as well as on the tomb of D. Gonzalo Fernandez de Cordova, El Gran Capitan of the Reyes Catolicos. He was put in charge of the new Renaissance project for the Cathedral.

The decision of the town council to change the style of the new Cathedral caused quite a stir and many misgivings within certain circles. Most important, however, was the King's disapproval, as stated in a Royal Order sent to the Cabildo at

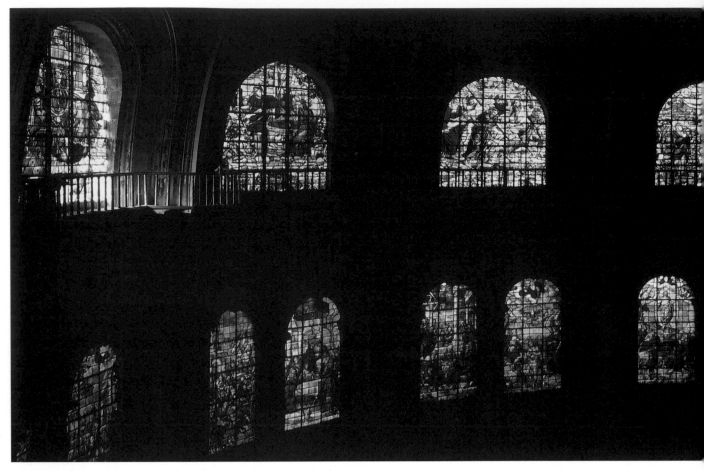

Stained glass of the main Chapel by Theodor van Holland & Johan van Kamp.

the end of 1528. Among other reasons the Monarch felt that the change in style would be detrimental to the Royal Chapel.

On the 9th of January 1529 Diego de Siloe, defended his project before the Monarch. His presentation was apparently successful, the new project was approved, and work continued on the new Cathedral . Siloe utilized the piers and pedestals of the pilasters in the exterior walls, the distribution of the transept and probably, the width and length of the original project. The changes made by Siloe in the rest of the foundation and the remaining structure are a clear example of a Renaissance church rising from a Gothic floor plan. The interior of the temple consists of five aisles supported by twenty enormous pillars, flanked by Corinthian columns that raise its dome to a height of 30 meters.

The Capilla Mayor is one of the most superb constructions of this kind in Spain. The circu-lar structure housing the high altar is the mas-terpiece of Siloe's work. It is extremely high, (45 meters) overwhelm ingly graceful, and transmits a luminous clarity. The cupola is sus-tained by twelve thick Corinthian pillars, which valiently adapt their arches to the curva-ture of the dome.

It is connected to the ambulatory by seven ope-nings between the piers, now closed by the choir which was placed around the altar in 1926. At that time it was moved from its usual position in the central aisle.

Siloe's solutions to technical problems, thanks to his genius, become aesthetic successes. The monumental nature of the main chapel, of colossal dimensions and intent, is in harmony and proportion thanks to the use of a series of modulating units; plinths, columns attached to pilasters and round arches, perfectly spaced up to the dome, with prominent ribs that accen-tuate the exactness of the space.

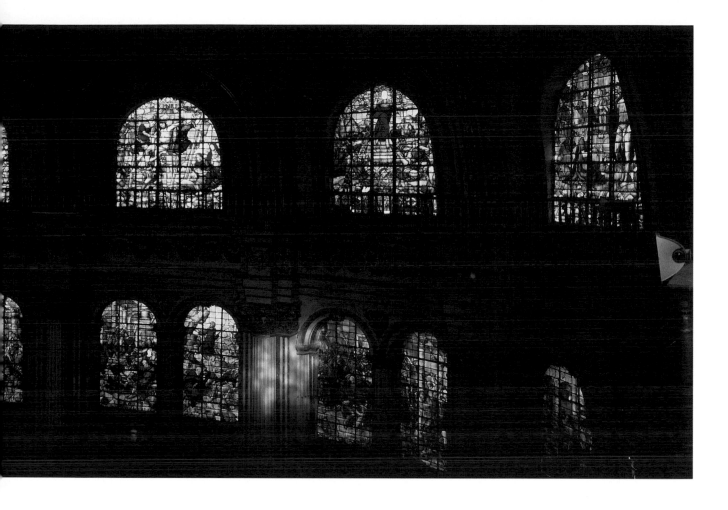

As is to be expected, especially inside, all of this area is covered with religious imagery. Affixed to the 12 columns of the chapel, in Baroque style, are the figures of the apostles, like the pillars upon which Christ built his Church. From the bottom to the top, including the stained glass windows, we have an iconographic interpretation of the Redemption of Christ. On the columns of the second level are seven large paintings by Alonso Cano of episodes in the life of the Virgin. The stained-glass windows from Flanders are painted in part by Theodore of Holland and include the Transfiguration, the Last Supper and the Cruci fixion .

The treatment of the entire chapel is a triumphal one, both in its architectural aspects as well as in its decoration.

The rest of Siloe's project is clearly Renaissance, both in its floor plan as well as in its elevation. The choir was placed in the center of the main aisle, as was the main transept; in front of the main chapel, at a tangent to the great circle of the dome, and crossing the temple at its widest point. The other transept is in the ambulatory, covering only three aisles. Siloe's project ends with a façade that has a triple triumphal arch and two towers.

Its clear conception is confirmed in its classic proportions and in the richness of its iconographic symbolism. Justifiably this monument is a model and example for other great Andalusian Renaissance ca thedrals.

The exterior beauty of the whole monument, especially the Main Chapel and ambulatory, was once a special part of the Granada landscape. Before it became surrounded by buildings that have destroyed its majesty, it once inspired poets and painters. A lovely drawing of its profile, by Velazquez gives us a clear picture of its grandiosity.

Vaults of the Cathedral.

THE PORTALS

Diego de Siloe, architect and sculptor, completed the monument with portals as rich in sculptural elements as in solutions to architectural composition. Such is the case with the Ecce Homo, in the Main Chapel, the entrance to the Sacristy and above all, the Puerta del Perdon, on the north side. This plateresque portal, done between 1535 and 1538 was completed almost a century before the main, or west portal designed by Alonso Cano, in Baroque style.

In the Puerta del Perdon with its noble proportions and fine artistic work we find one of Siloe's loveliest creations. Above the central arch we have the figures of Faith and Justice, considered by some, the best of Siloe's work.

The tablet between the two figures bears the following inscription: "After 700 years of Moslem domination, we both (Faith and Justice) gave these dominions to the Catholic Sovereigns: within this temple are their bodies and their souls have gone to heaven, because they acted with justice and faith"

On the lateral pillars are shields held by angels; on the right, the imperial crest of Carlos V and on the left the crest of the Catholic Monarchs.

Until his death in 1563 Siloe remained in charge of the work, completing the Capilla

Mayor and ambulatory and beginning the naves from the transept. The first mass was celebrated in 1561. In 1666 almost a century later, in the Baroque period, the main entrance was created by Alonso Cano. Cano's design, continued after his death by Jose Granados de la Barrera, and later by Melchor de Aguirre at the end of the 18th century, is roughly a Roman triumphal arch with its impressive central entrance flanked by smaller arches on each side. Its well proportioned masses stand out boldly, giving the chiaroscuro effect that Cano so often achieved in his paintings. Cano conceived the portal as a great retablo in which the sculptural elements and decorative ones play a double roll: the iconographic and the dynamic aesthetic one.

The assorted sculpture is mostly by Verdiguier and his son.

All of this work belongs to a moment in the history of the church when the monumental nature of the exterior was used to attract the attention and emotion of the faithful, thus creating a holy space in the plaza that stands before the temple.

THE INTERIOR DECORATION

All the unrestrained feeling of the facade is found in the interior of the Cathedral in its rich collection of Baroque retablos of the XVIII century, among which stand out the unique piece by Duque Cornejo of Nuestra

Panorama of the naves of the Cathedral from the Second floor of the Main Chapel..

Inmaculate Conception by Alonso Cano.

Senora de la Antigua; one of Santiago; the one of the altar of Jesus of Nazareth, all profusely gilded and with original design in sculpture as well as painting.

Also of note, are the large Baroque organs and pulpits. worked in marble and engraved in gold by the architect Francisco Hurtado Izquierdo, and the magnificent marble and polychromed retablo of Nuestra Señora de las Angustias.

Neoclassicism is represented by three retablos of impor-tance: la Virgen del Pilar, by Francisco Aguado in 1785; those in the Chapel of San Cecilio, dedicated to the patron Saint of the city, and those to the copatrons San Juan de Dios, on the right, and to San Emigidio (defender against earthquakes) on the left, also designed by Francisco Aguado and sculpted by Verdiguier. The static equilibrium of the neoclassic works appear as a chapter in parenthesis next to the Baroque and the elegance of the whole Cathedral.

The work of Alonso Cano as painter and sculptor, stands out in this monument. Among all his works, and possibly the most appealing in this cathedral, is a miniature carved Inmaculada.

Today in the Sacristy. it was originally made for the lectern in the choir, and is one of the key pieces of the Spanish Baroque period.

It is not possible here to try to point out all of the painted works and canvases in this cathedral. We can only suggest the importance of this monument as a center of Renaissance and Baroque art.

Polychromed sculpture of Saint Paul by Alonso Cano.

31

Wideangle view of the interior of the Cathedral.

OTHER MONUMENTS

Renaissance Granada is also represented by many other civil and religious monuments. The Palace of Castril (today the Provincial Archeological Museum), the Royal Hospital or the lovely portal of the Lonja, to name a few, are all illustrative of the Plateresque style. While the impressive Palaces of Calahorra and Carlos V of the Alhambra are defined as examples of renaissance architecture in its purest forms.

The completion of the Royal Chapel in 1521. at tracted many of the best national and international artists who were enthusiastic about the new Romanesque style. Masters such as Alonso de Berruguete, Jacobo Florentino and Pedro Machuca, painter. author and architect of the Palace of Carlos V of the Alhambra, had come to

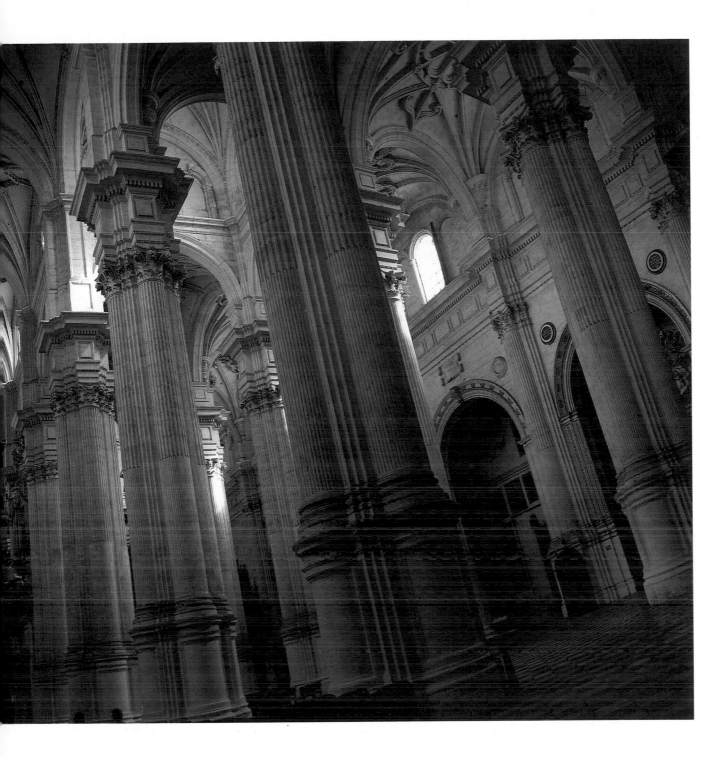

Granada, interested in the works in progress in the new imperial city.

The Emperor, Carlos V, in 1526 came with his bride, Isabel de Portugal. They arrived with an entourage that included ambassadors, diplomats, secretaries, ladies-in-waiting, artists, poets...

All had come to the new Christian city to see at first hand the marvels that were being created here. Diego de Siloe was also here in charge of the building of the church of San Jerónimo. In 1521 a Royal decree had granted the Gran Capitan's wife, the use of this new temple as the final resting place for this great national hero and leader.

In essence, but on a larger scale, the floor plan repeats the form of the Royal Chapel's sanctuary. Both in the location of the transept as well as in the form of the nave and its chapels.

Main facade of the Cathedral by Alonso Cano.

Originally conceived in Gothic style it was continued by Jacobo Florentino in Renaissance style, employing in the interior ribbed Corinthian pilasters and outside grouping the buttresses in pyramidal form with modular structures and cornices.

In 1528 Siloe was called to take charge of the works. Commissioned to close the sanctuary, he was given total freedom in the planning of all architectural, sculptural and artistic work in the temple. He began with the second floor plan of the temple although his greatest innovation was the completion of the transept. The cupola is mounted on four ribbed arches on which are the figures of the four Evangelists from which spring four flared arches. While the style is not at all classic, it is harmonious and balanced. These stylistic solutions inside, combined with the exterior work (spaced buttresses, triple arched windows, coat-of-arms and figures), all create a monument, which shares its religious function with its vigorous desire to glorify the memory of El Gran Capitan. The figurative themes of the sculptures and the

tablets with their inscriptions, all accentuate this intention .

En 1547 Siloe contracted the choir stalls and still with some Gothic elements, created a lovely pair of portals for the large cloister completed in 1519. He also completed the fine ornamentation at the base of the main fasade and of the tower. This tower was dismantled by the French at the beginning of the XIX century in order to construct a bridge. In 1963 the Director General of Fine Arts ordered the reconstruction of the tower.

Siloe's work, as well as that of Jacobo Florentino, must be esteemed both for its architectural and sculptural aspects. From what was originally meant to be a humble Gothic church, they created one of the finest examples of Spanish Renaissance.

The polygonal sanctuary is decorated on the exterior with lovely cornices on the buttresses

Panoramic view of the city from the roof of the Cathedral and the shield of the Gate of Pardon.

View of the Cathedral from the Corral de la Lona in Albaicín.

and sculptural groupings of giant Roman soldiers who bear the coats-of-arms of the founders. On the upper level there are two lovely figures representing Fortitude and Industry. They hold a large tablet which reveals the purpose of this monument. On it we read: "Gonzalo Fernández de Cordova great leader of the Spanish and terror of the French and the Turks". At each side there is a medallion with the portraits of El Gran Capitan and his wife. These same themes were repeated indoors but they were unfortunately covered by XVIII century paintings.

On the domes of the transept and of the sanctuary, Siloe developed an iconographic work which glorifies the memory of the founders, buried in the church. In high relief he represents the heroes and heroines of antiquity, whose deeds he recalls and compares with those of El Gran Capitan and his wife. Here we see the figures of Caesar, Hannibal, Pompey, Mark, Homer and other heroines, as well as Abigail, Judith, Deborah, Penelope and other heroes.

36

View of the City from Avenue of the Constitution.

On the coffers of the sanctuary's dome are represented the Savior, the Apostles, Angels and in relief there are several saints and the warrior saints. George, Sebastian, Martin and others. All this is featured in honour of El Gran Capitan and his wife.

Completing this monument is the Monastery of the same name with its two lovely cloisters, rich portals, and the coat-of-arms of the first archbishop of Granada, the monk Fray Hernando de Talavera, and of the Catholic Monarchs.

The most important sculptural piece of Andalusian Baroque art is the great "Retablo" of the main altar. It was contracted in 1570 to the painter Juan de Aragon who was assisted by the Granadine sculptor Melchor de Turín and the art studio of Vazquez el Joven. The

Alcaicería, the old silk Market

37

design was modified in 1573 and amplified in 1603. The whole of the Retablo, with its lovely gold tones completes the presbytery, offering us, as a whole, one of the loveliest images that XVII century Granada can offer.

There are many Renaissance portals of Mudejar churches in the city that bear the particular mark of Siloe's style. Clear examples of this are the portals of the churches of Santa Ana, S. Matias, el Salvador, S. Miguel, San Andres, S. Ildefonso and even the lovely building of the ancient University, today the Ecclesiastic Curia, closed because of a recent fire.

The Chancellory of Granada, work of Francisco del Castillo, with its rich historical legacy, closes and opens the transition from Renaissance to Baroque. It is, as a whole, but especially its façade, one of the most noble and monumental works of its time.

In 1500 the Catholic Monarchs initiated a judicial reform which included the transfer of one of the Royal Tribunals from Castille to Granada. By 1525 the available facilities proved inadecuate and the King decreed that a new residence should be built. Thus, this magnificent building with its imposing central patio, in which we find Siloe's influence, was built. The monumental stairway and the facade, however, were not begun until 1578 and 1587, respectively. By the end of the century the Chancellory was so well known in all of Spain that its beauty and originality were mentioned in literary works of the period.

The main entrance is topped by a sculptured marble slab, framed by a split pediment and supported by a lion. On it, in part, is inscribed in Latin: "May the Justice despensed herein be equal to the offense committed...". In the center and completing the façade is the Royal coat-of-arms, and at its sides and resting on the divided pediment are the statues of Justice and Fortitude.

When evaluating this facade we should mention the original distribution of the openings. All seems to be vertically linked, a fact which is accented by the contrast of the beveled stone with the flat stone. Contrasting the seven vertical groupings are the two horizontal cornices, one halfway with a small projection and the other at the top with a greater overhang. These cornices accentuate the semi-circular and triangular pediments of the seven balconies. All of the other openings including the first floor windows offer us with their curves and counter-curves a clear indicative of a pre-baroque style, also evident in the rich chromatic effect produced by the mixtures of grey, white and green marble.

The monumental nature of this building was justified because of the function it performed, as well as the history of this institution, which administered justice in Andalucia from 1505 to 1834.

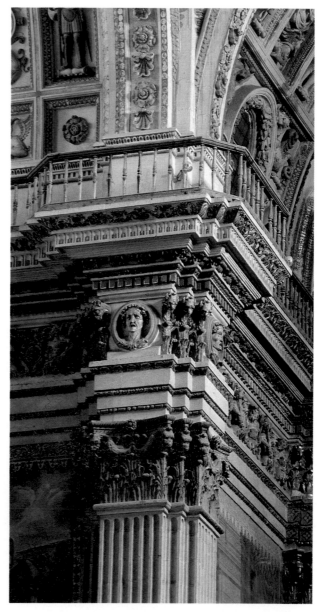

Pillar of the transept in the church of Saint Jerónimo by Diego de Siloé.

38

Transept and high altar of the church of San Jerónimo.

In general, this solemn building sets before the plaza which is in front of it an image that clearly speaks of the greatness of Renaissance and baroque Granada. A period which was to be completed with other great baroque portals, retablos and altar niches such as the Diputación, the Law School (originally the Jesuit school of San Pablo), the Notary College and the churches of St. Justo and S. Pastor or of S. Juan de Dios or the Basilica of Nuestra Senora de las Angustias.

Dr. D. Pedro Salmerón Escobar

41

Ca. 1.900

Chancillería.

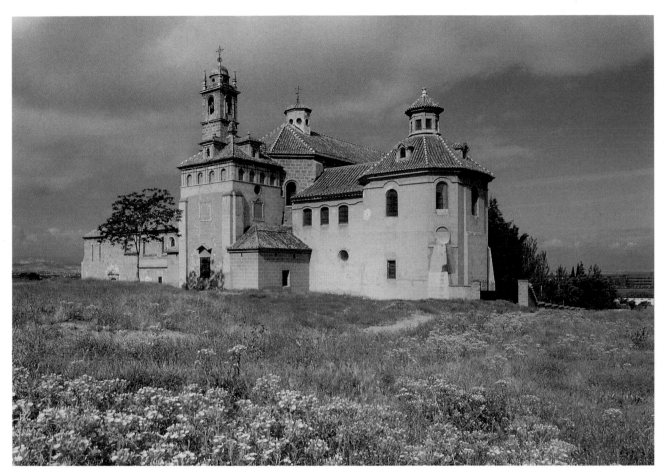

The Carthusian Monastery.

THE CARTHUSIAN MONASTERY

The monastery of la Cartuja, with its church, tabernacle, sacristy and other dependencies, is the monument which most clearly expresse what the Baroque style was in Granada. Founded in 1492 at the time of the Reconquest, it contains examples of Gothic, Renaissance and Plateresque; but all that which was done in Baroque style, during the XVII and XVIII centuries, is that which attains a superior level of quality, and within Spanish Baroque, great originality. In many ways this can be considered the culmination of Andalucian Baroque and the most profound and expressive example of religious asceticism and mysticism in the life of the Carthusian monks.

In order to fully understand what this monument means in the life of the Order, one must first have an understanding of its location and surroundings.

Outside of the city, it is but a kilometre from the Puerta de Elvira and in a place where nature brimmed with beauty. During the reign of the Moors it was a place of orchards, carmenes (granadine villas), and many vine yards, with abundant water from the fountains of Alfacar. It was a

fertile land with flourishing gardens as described by Ibn Aljatib. It was a beautiful landscape covered with gardens. Today our imagination must take flight because of the great urban aspect of the surrounding area. The enclosed property of the monastery, however, allows us to imagine the once lovely gardens that were housed there. According to a XVII century historian, this spot was chosen for the monastery as a result of an initial contribution made by El Gran Capitan. It appears that he was at this spot when defending himself against the moors and he later expressed his desire to be buried here in a church. First located on a hill it presented many difficulties to the first Carthusian builders, so much so that it was moved to an area of lower ground. As a result of this move El Gran Capitan became disinterested in the project and left it in the hands of the founders.

Sancta Sanctorum

The move was approved in 1514 and the work was left in the hands of Fray Alonso de Ledesma, who projected the dependencies around a great cloister, 53 metres long, with a cemetery in the center, then a large garden and a Claustrillo (little cloister), which is the one that exists today. Around this Claustrillo was the Refectory, the Chapter House, the "Profundis" chamber and small chapels. Around the large Cloister the monks built cells which no longer exist.

The church, was erected upon a foundation made in the XVI and XVII centuries by the quarrier Cristobal de Vilchez. The Claustrillo was made at the same time and completed during the first quarter of the XVII century. According to the Carthusian historian Jose de Valles, four towers were planned, two at the foot and two at the head, of which only the one at the right of the epistolary was completed. It seems that it was a later idea to construct the Chapel of the Sagrario in the center of the sanctuary, as well as the great sacristy which was connected to the left of the same. At the end of the XVIII century in 1794, the Neoclassic portal was made, the work of the Hermoso brothers, Joaquin the archtect and Pedro Antonio the sculptor of San Bruno, in white marble. At the back of an ample courtyard, which is reached through a Plateresque doorway, attributed to Juan Garcia de Prades, is the majestic façade of the church, high atop a broad double Baroque staircase. The sober Neoclassic portal, of grey marble stands out upon the honey coloured stone of the rest of the façade. On top of the entrance, as a royal foundation, is the coat-of-arms of Spain. Contrasting with this cultured image is the granadine stone pavement of the courtyard, covered with hunting scenes and the shield of Spain with the date 1679.

THE CLAUSTRILLO AND ITS SECTIONS

Today's entrance to the Monastery is through the claustrillo, just a simple patio with arches and with columns from the Doric style, opens into the garden and whose focal point is a fountain. A modern and well done restoration left it open, so creating a monastic atmosphere fitting in with the functions carried out in the XVII century, because in this way, the Refectory, the De Profundis, the Friars Chapter, the Monks Chapter and the north side, a series of chapels for intimate prayer and meditation, and the two doors to the church, all communicate with it.

For these sections -Claustrillo and the attached rooms- built in the XVI century and of gothic style with lovely ribbed vaults, expansive spaces harmoniously proportioned, Juan Sanchez Cotan drew a true chronicle of the Order; he was a laybrother of the Fraile Chapter, born in Orgaz in the province of Toledo in 1560 where he became a painter and who had come to this Cartuja in 1603. Near his works we find another series, also in the form of a chronicle, of the painter Vicente Carducho, replicas of those which he painted for the Monasterio del Paular. All of them represent the history of the Order, from the death of Diocres in Paris, which motivated in St. Bruno and his companions the decision to establish the Order, up to the martyrdom scenes suffered by the monks in England during the epoch of Enrique VIII and in other parts of

Europe at the hands of the Turks and the Huguenots.

The naturalism of the paintings, especially those by Sanchez Cotan, intentionally fill these silent spaces and invite the characters to emerge from their canvases, with their beautiful white robes in order to assist the Chapter and attend to the call of the church bells. So they become true illustrations of the live architectural texts and the monastic life, because they were painted for very concrete places of these sections; it is through them and through their apparent realism that we can see their trascendental idealism.

The monks who prayed, studied and worked in this monastery, daily were able to realize their "visible talking". Such is the case of the presence of the first community of Christ with his apostles in the Last Supper, painted in the Refectory around 1618 and where the light projected above the cenacle is just the same as the real light which penetrates through the lateral windows and illuminates and casts shadows on the abstinent dishes that are on the table. Another example is the representation of the martyr's exemplary heroism who died defending their faith, showing an example of value and confidence in God.

In these sense, the bithematic and narrative canvasses have a special didactic value, now grouped in the Refectory and Chapter rooms, some of them related to the life of St. Bruno and others to these martyrdom scenes.

Choir of the brothers.

It was probably here where Sanchez Cotan made one of the first rnonastic painting collections in Spain. A chapter which, during the XVII century, was abundant especially in Andalucia where the religious orders looked for, in these realistic series of deeds of a saint or merits of an order, the ideal ocassion to estimulate their own life of prayer and meditation in the monastic interiors.

The paintings, which were destined for the walls of the convent, were big canvasses and not frescos made for covering great spaces. For this reason, as professor Julian Gallego noted, "when these canvasses are taken from the place for which they were meant for and the displayed isolated in museums- as has happened with some of them- they cease to express the intention of their painters It is certain that in these monastic collections there is a programmatic, didactic and even rethoric idea, which inspires the election and arrangements of the themes".

Thus, each painting is valued not only by itself, but in relation with the rest of the series, and each series is articulately explained in the entire house.

Ceiling of the Sacristy. Down: Saint Bruno.

Nowadays, the series in the Cartuja of Granada—except those transferred to the Bellas Artes museums—are gathered in the Refectory Room, where the bithematic canvasses dedicated to the martyrdom works of Sanchez Cotan area highlighted; in the Chapter Room, the Aparicion de la Virgen a St. Bruno on his deathbed, the miracles of his sepulchre and other works by Vicente Carducho are the focal point.

In the De Profundis Room, which served as prayer and mortuary chapel built in 1600 next to the Refectory, the friar laybrother painted an altarpiece with the figures of St. Peter and St. Paul and a landscape in the background; all of it showing a wide display of relief and visual effects, both being characteristics very common in the paintings at the end of the manneristic and the beginning of the naturalistic periods.

This tendency is also evident in the simple wooden cross, which with a minute detail of realism, the author has painted over the Last Supper in the Refectory Room. These "trompe d'oeil" were common in the paintings of the Cartujas.

In the small chapels in the north side are two important pieces of the Baroque art of Granada. One of them is an impressive Ecce Homo, in multicoloured fired clay; it is a work of the Garda brothers- Miguel and Jeronimo- at the end of the XVI century, a half torso, to be contemplated and meditated closely in the intimacy of a small chapel (this work didn't belong to the Cartuja).

The other piece, a lovely image of the Virgen del Rosario by Jose Risueño, shows with a natural expression a beautiful Child in her arms who smilingly faces the onlooker. These certainly are two pieces that justify not only the function of intimate space in the baroque chapel, but also their own level of naturalism present in the works that here fulfilled a function of real and bodily nearness to the image of the sacred. For these chapels Sanchez Cotan also painted some canvasses, which are today in the Museum and in private collections,

THE CHURCH

The Church, composed of only one groundplant, was erected in the XVII century by Cristobal de Vilchez. The profuse decoration of its walls with plastered motifs of rich vegetation, produces impressions of spacial dynamism, accentuated with exhalted baroquism by the presence of zenithal light which contrast with the rhythm and reliefs; another factor is the predominant whiteness of the group only matched with the colours in the canvas of the series about the Life of the Virgin, painted in 1676 especially for this temple by the painter Pedro Atanasio Bocanegra of Granada, a disciple of Alonso Cano.

As a Carthusian church, its floor space is divided into three parts, each one according to a type of attendants: the first one is for believers in general, in the middle is the choir for the monks; these divisions don't interrupt the overall spacial continuity of the temple; the first part is separated by a simple metal grill, and the separation of the choirs is done with a lovely combination of two low retables with a glass and marquetery door, a work of the brother Vazquez.

In this way, all the decorative and figurative elements accentuate a rhythm which focuses towards the head where a baldachin altar, graceful and brilliant with gold and mirrors, is highlighted it was made in 1710 by Francisco Hurtado Izquierdo with a image of the Asuncion carved by Jose de Mora, supple and looking upwards.

This combination communicates to the inside of the temple a high level of dynamism which transforms the ambience into something etherial and sublime. At the back, iconographically represented is the mystery of the Asuncion de la Virgen on two canvasses.Below, the apostles next to the vacant sepulcher, and above in the arcade of the ellipsoidal cupola the triumphant representation of the Virgin, lifted by the angels towards the heavens.

The intensity of the presbytery colours makes the focal point even more attractive and transforms it into the point where everything converges.

The space occupied by the Shrine, as the main chapel, centers in its darkness a background that becomes concave by its own transparency.

Together with this sensation of dynamism also abounds the impression of wealth which is greatly contributed by the two beautiful side retables made in the XVII century with canvases of Sanchez Cotan. On the right the Baptism of Christ and on the left The Rest on the Flight to Egypt; this last work is one of the finest belonging to the first epoch of the painter, and where the elegance and sobriety of the composition is accompanied by the fine treatment of the pictorial theme especially manifested in the still life where some bread and cheese are placed on a white tablecloth spread on the flowered covered grass, everything singing of the beauty and the trascendent contents of nature itself, which, as the poet affirms, is not dead here.

Completing the presbytery and at the end of the left of the monks choir, is a beautiful retable (between 1730-1736) framing a canvas of the Virgen del Rosario by Pedro Atanasio Bocanegra and which reigns over the monks devotion in the choir and which is artistically the most expressive and communicative work of the disciple of Cano.

BAROQUISM AND SYMBOLISM IN THE SHRINE OF HURTADO IZQUIERDO

The overall attraction which the monument offers, as a monastic ambient for silence and meditation, arrives at its most important chapter with the execution of this singular piece of the Spanish Baroque and which is the Sancta Sanctorum of the Cartuja.

It seems, according to the known records, that the idea of its construction was probably decided in the middle of the XVII century and before finishing the decoration of the church because the presbytery's ornamental distribution alludes and frames the entrance to the interior of this new space that becomes the authentic nucleus, the center and final point of the whole cult of the temple; it also becomes one of the most exalted examples of the Spanish Baroque, magnificent in its movements and gestures and at the same time in harmony with the ensemble thanks to the plastic and colourful mobility of the different arts represented here in a pleasing harmony due to the creative idea and the deep argumental contents integrated in the whole. The architectural structure was initiated in 1702 according to the project and direction of the famous architect Francisco Hurtado Izquierdo, from the city of Lucena, and already known for his important works in Cordoba. The simplicity of the floor plan is resolved with a square which, resting on four arches, holds a cupola placed over trapezoidal pechinas together with lateral chapels which in ther turn reinforce and complete it; once in the interior there is an extremely beautiful conjunction of the supportive and decorative elements with an unique profusion of rich marbles, bright golden carvings, luminous frescos and oil paintings together with the iconographic and dynamic compliment of naturalistic sculptures which complete the architectonic plastic.

Everything here is in the state of effervescence, dynamized in the structures and decorative surfaces. Nothing remains static, and for a more intense call to the senses, it seems as if the law of physics was inverted and the sustaining elements, the eight columns which occupy the four square angles and are mounted on complicated baroque styled plinths were hiding with their dark tones in front of the brilliant golds of the bases and capitals.

The vertical repetition of its fluted shafts is in contrast with the curved profiles of the sculptures placed among them and even more with the pavillions which lodge them crowned by angels who with their chromatism and ingravity contribute to their continous contrast. All the mouldings of the entablature, the frames of the paintings and the base of the cupola are outlined with ondulating lines, which dynamize even more the already existing mouldings. Centering in the lateral sides, on the bottom parts, are open intrepid oculos which connect with the two chapels, framed by curves and spirals and mouldings, sculptured in polished red marble, over which are placed the allegories, wood carved and richly polychromed a small branch of alberchiqus in his hand, a consecrated bush in the ancient times of Hippocrates, the god of science. Corresponding to this allegory an interpretation of the scene of Christ in the house of Martha and Martha is offered, as being the symbol of silence in the contemplative life.

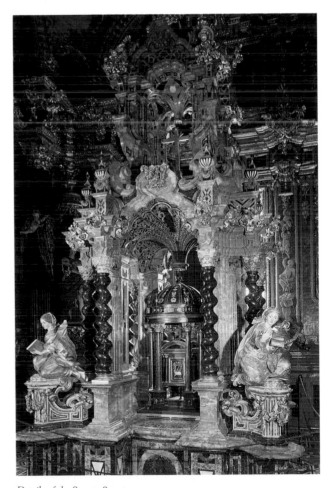

Details of the Sancta Sanctorum

49

The allegory of Solitude, situated in front of Silence, is a clear reference to life in the cell; here it is represented by a matron dressed in white with a solitary bird on her head, a book in her right hand for study and meditation and under her left arm a hare, an example of a solitary animal. In connection with this allegory Palomino has painted a medallion with the supper of Emaus as a reference to the Eucharist and the lonely life of the withdrawn disciples and pilgrims. Finally, the four pechinas are occupied by the images of the four Evangelists.

All this program continues throughout the rest of the shrine, as much in the paintings as in the sculptures. In the entrance, the King-Prophet David is painted in the jambs; he is the ascendent of the Redeemer, and his posture points towards the tabernacles; he also bears the palmist lire. In the opposite jamb Melchisedech is presented offering bread with both hands and a pitcher of wine at his feet, establishing a clear precedent of Jesus Christ's priesthood in relation to the Eucharist.

On the sides, next to one another, centered on the wall there are two enormous paintings also by Palomino both with themes referring to the premonition and announcement of the Eucharist in the Old Testament. Thus, on the right side there is a scene which shows Moses with his prodigious staff, defending himself from the angel who is trying to kill his son with a sword; to avoid it, Sefora, his mother, circumcises him. Symbolically Moses represents Christ who has become the husband of the Church through the sacrifice of the Calvary which is renewed in the Eucharist. Above this painting is the scene of David being given the sword of Goliath. In the lower part, sculptured, the allegories of the monastic virtues of the compunction with the mounth open and a heart crowned with thorns in the left hand and pointing to the heavens with the right. To its side, the virtue of Charity or the Love of God with a burning heart in its hand.

On the opposite wall there is also an Eucharistic prefiguration with the scene of Abigail offering gifts of bread, wine and a calf, to David so as to placate her anger against her husband Nabal. Above, the Purification of Isalas, known as the circumcision of the lips sculptured and on the pedestal are the allegories of the monastic virtues, done by Duque Cornejo; one of them is Obedience who bears a yoke in one hand and a crucifix in the other. At its side is Vigilance with a book in one hand and a lit candle in the other. At its side is a crane with the lifted claw sustaining a rock which doesn't allow him to fall asleep.

According to the peculiarity of the Carthusian life, are seen the symbols referring to a hermetical and cenobitical life, or communal life and solitary life in the cell.

This main cell, symbolic and unique, is covered by a cupola where Palomino offers the triumphante celestial of the Eucharist in the exhalted monstrance - which here substitutes the Mystic Lamb- and presides over the terrestial globe that St. Bruno holds as an atlantis. Palomino writes in conclusion: "By that token the whole recint becomes the expression of a militant church and most especially is a panegyric of the holy Carthusian religion, based on the silence, contemplation and doctrine; these are the triumphant Jerusalem, represented in the Glory expressed in the entire ambient of the cupola; and thus, the essence of this blessed community rise as the greatest gift to the Lords Sovereign". On the base of the cupola,

appears the Monastic Religion, represented as a grand matron with a veil over her face, carrying some cilices and disciplines. In relation to this allegory is the scene of Christ fasting in the desert and the subsequent help from the angels with regards to the Carthusian life and to the Eucharist. The allegory of Silence is represented by an elder with his finger on his mouth and a quacking duck at his side, but the duck has a rock in its beak which prevents it from quacking.

All this monument of entrances and exits are compensed in his ground space with the small central, niche, which appears as a great marble monstrance, the axis and reason of the whole iconographic and dynamic content of this chapel, being the place where everything converges and where originally the primitive tabernacle, was placed a beautiful urn made of bright silver is like a transparent crystal from where the monument triumphantly rises which as a fountain of bliss and culminates firstly in the redempting cross, and lastly with the image of the Faith which seems to be due to the optic of the painting, embedded in the dome.

The conclusion is, as the Professor Orozco Diaz affirms, "that as in all the great baroque works, the most extraordinary flattery and sensorial excitation, can take, by this way of the appearance of the senses to suggest the grandest and most transcendental religious spirit".

But inside all this language of the forms, integrated by the various arts, there is a complete iconographic and symbolic discourse which transforms this room into a beautiful synthesis of what it signifies for the Cartuja the cult of the Eucharist as the triumphant right where the love of God is manifested towards mankind.

in painted figures and medallions, are represented a series of allegories and scenes referring to the Eucharist. The Faith, as the foundation of the Eucharistic mystery and the monastic life, is represented by a figure with a cartel which says, "Blessed are those who didn't see but believed" in relation to it, in the adjoining medallion, the historic institution, of the sacrament in the Last Supper: In Front of the Faith

The Carthusian Order, since its General Chapter in 1261, ordered a special distribution of its churches in such a way that all its parts were to be in spacial and visual contact with the shrine, thus becoming the center of the cult.

On the far wall there is a window, with an important function of lighting the room. On both sides are the allegories of **Peace and Gentleness**, the first crowned with a laurel and the second with a meek lamb which substitutes the symbolic elephant, the most common attribute of this virtue. In the central niche this symbolic-iconographic discourse is com-

The Sacristy.

pleted with four virtues and monastic qualifications which are: **Veritas**, with a rich diadem on his forehead and an open book; **Integritas**, with a tablet with Arabic numbers: **Examen**, with a clepsydra or a water clock, and **Esca**, or food, with a fish referring to the rigour of the fast and the abstinence for Carthusian life. These virtues, are carved in wood, based on models by Duque Cornejo, and are richly polychromed in gold which makes them more dynamic and supple. The four great figures which occupy the angular intercolumnation are, St. John the Baptist, by Risueño; the Magdalene by Duque Cornejo; St. Bruno and St. Joseph by Jose de Mora, likewise complete this iconographic collection the first three representing the penitent and the anchorite life, and St. Joseph as an example of a silent and secluded life.

Thus, and in conclusion, this magnificent baroque piece offers two complementary discourses to understand: a plastic one, with a dynamism of forms, lights and colours and the erudit and symbolic discourse whose manifestations give the image of the Eucharistic triumph, and further more the syrnbolic cell, and Carthusian ideal for the Eucharistical Christ.

THE SACRISTY

Outside of the Sagrario and to the left of the presbytery we see before us doors of Taracea (inlaid with ivory, ebony and tortose shell).

An impressive spectacle of Andalusian Baroque architecture

which creates fantastic effects of light and perspective. On the 5th of January 1713 the construction of the Sacristy was authorized and it is assumed that because of his success with El Sagrario, Francisco Hurtado Izquierdo also planned the first steps of the new work, although there is no record of who directed the project.

The most important period was from 1741-1747 during which time all the interior stucco work, the three foot dado of veined brown marble and the paving were completed. There are many suppositions as to who were the masters who created this work but no document reveals with certainty its authors.

Once more, a key work in the history of art, both for its style, as well as its type, remains anonymous. This unique work, different from all others of the same type, such as the Sagrario of the church of S. Mateo by Leonardo Antonio de Castro or the Sagrario of the parish of Priego de Pedrajas. Aesthetically, this work utilizes the effects of perspective and light. Space, illuminated from the sides or from above, make the chiaroscuro of the carved white adornments dynamic outlined in blue to project spaces and profiles. Everything seems to sprout from the veined and intensely contrasting marble of the dado. The pavement, in black and white diamond shaped marble, increases the dynamic space and seems to remove the background to a distance, creating an environment without static references.

This unreal world into which we are drawn is the perfect backdrop for appreciating the ecstasy of the small statue of St. Bruno by Jose de Mora. This unique example of plastic mysticism closes our visit to one of the most important chapters in Christian and Baroque Granada.

Domingo Sanchez Mesa

Professor of History.

Art University of Granada

Cenete

Calahorra (Patio)

Bayárcal

Montefrío

El Charcón

56

Edición: J. Agustín Núñez. EDILUX
Diseño: Germán Madinabeitia
Fotografía: J. Agustín Núñez & Miguel Román
Impresión: Croma
Fotomecánica: Franacolor
Dep. Legal: 823 - 1996
ISBN: 84-87282-83-0